The Art of the KNIFE

The Art of the KNIFE

No portion of this book may be
reproduced by any means without
permission in writing by the publisher.

Printed in USA

© Copyright 2013 KitchenAdvance

ISBN 978-1-938653-17-9

The Art of the KNIFE

APPETIZERS

SALADS

The Art of the KNIFE

Table of Contents

The Art of the KNIFE

The Art of the KNIFE

The Art of the KNIFE

INTRODUCTION

The Art of the KNIFE

The Knife...One of Man's Oldest Tools

The knife is an amazing tool – an ancient tool for which there has been no substitute. Throughout history, knives have been essential for survival, as well as for providing food and shelter. From its earliest form, the knife developed out of necessity, and its evolution may be traced through the paths of technology.

The knives used in the kitchen today are remarkably like the ones developed thousands of years ago. During the Stone Age, knives were made of flint, which could easily be scaled to shape, and then could be re-scaled to produce a new edge. Later, flint knives were ground to the desired shape. Much later in history, man began to make knives from copper, bronze, and finally, from iron.

As knife technology and production methods have advanced, knife uses have expanded and knife forms have become more specialized. Today, you can get a knife in a wide assortment of configurations and materials. Technical advances and research into the construction of knives has led to refinements of metal alloys, the ability to refine an edge to a specific task and all sorts of adjustments to shape and construction of a blade to prevent fatigue and stress.

Today, the knife continues to be an important tool, though more for sport and work than survival, as in the past. During all these years, however, the basics of a good tool's shape and function and the skills necessary to use tools have remained constant.

Types of Knives

CHEF'S KNIFE

The Chef's knife or French knife is the most often used knife in the kitchen. The blade shape is useful for peeling, trimming, slicing, chopping, mincing, filleting fish, and cutting meats and poultry. In

the hands of a skilled user, the Chef's knife can be used to perform the tasks of many special purpose knives.

UTILITY KNIFE

This is a smaller version of the Chef's knife and can be used for light cutting, peeling and slicing tasks. The blade is usually 5 to 7 inches

long. The blade is not only shorter, but thinner than the Chef's knife, so it makes this knife very useful for slicing small items, like tomatoes.

PARING KNIFE

The paring knife is the second most often used knife in the kitchen. With its 2 to 4-inch blade, this knife is used primarily for paring and

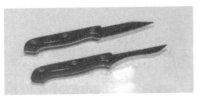

trimming vegetables and fruits. Blades can taper to a point much like a chef's knife, or they can curve or bend at the tip, which is sometimes referred to as a granny knife.

BONING KNIFE

A boning knife is used to separate raw meat from the bone. The blade

is about 6 inches long and is shorter and thinner than the blade of a chef's knife.

FILLETING KNIFE

The filleting knife is specifically used for filleting fish. This knife is similar in shape and size to the boning knife but has a more flexible

blade to allow easier separation of delicate flesh off the bone.

SLICER

The long, thin, narrow blade of the slicer allows the cutting of smooth slices in a single stroke. The type of edge and rigidity of

the blade depends on the type of food you are slicing. The tip can be pointed or round.

CLEAVER

The rectangular blade of the cleaver makes them perfect for the same applications as a chef's knife. They vary in size and heft

and the edge may be curved or straight, depending on the intended use.

SCIMITAR

The scimitar has a long curved blade about 12 to 16 inches in

length which makes is useful for slicing through large cuts of raw meat.

The Art of the KNIFE

Basic Knife Grips

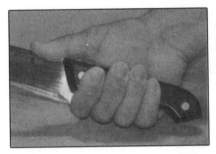

Grip the handle with four fingers and hold the thumb firmly against the blade's spine.

Grip the handle with all four fingers and hold the thumb gently but firmly against the side of the blade.

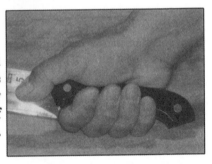

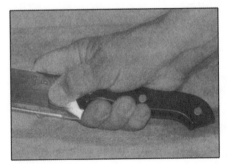

Grip the handle with three fingers, rest the index finger flat against the blade on one side, and hold the thumb on the opposite side to give additional stability and control.

The Guiding Hand

In this classic position, the fingertips are tucked under slightly to hold objects in place with thumb held back from fingertips. Knife blade rests against knuckles, preventing fingers from being cut.

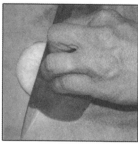

When peeling or trimming hold food in the air, above cutting surface. The guiding hand holds and turns the food against the blade.

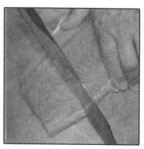

Butterflying meats or slicing a bagel in half call for the guiding hand to be placed on top of the food to keep it from slipping, while the cut is made into the food at a parallel or at an angle to the work surface.

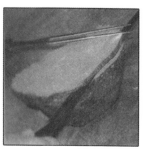

Use the guiding hand to hold a carving or kitchen fork while disjointing or carving cooked meats and poultry. Lay the tines of the fork flat on the surface or inserted directly into the item to hold it in place as it is carved.

The Art of the KNIFE

PRELIMINARY CUTS

Many foods require some preliminary trimming, peeling or squaring off to make subsequent cuts easier to perform.

Removing roots and stems from fruits, herbs and vegetables are among trimming tasks. A chef's knife works nicely for this task.

Peeling can be done with a rotary peeler if the skin is not too thick on foods such as carrots and potatoes or other similar skinned items. These peelers work in both directions.

Paring knives are used to peel and trim many vegetables and fruits.

18

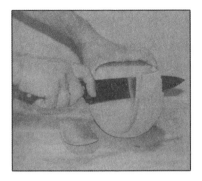

Use a chef's knife for vegetables and other foods with thick rinds or skins, such as hard skinned squashes, pineapples or melons.

Naturally round foods, such as this potato, are easier to control when cutting if you first remove a slice from the bottom or side, or cut in half to make it sit flat on the cutting surface.

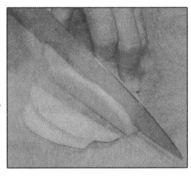

CHOPPING

Chopping means that food is cut into pieces that are roughly the same size, but it is not critical to cut them to the exact dimension called for when you dice or julienne an item.

Chopping is sometimes used interchangeably with mincing, but the distinction is that minced foods are generally cut to a finer size because the food itself is relatively fine, such as with the fresh herbs on the following page. Trim root and stem ends and slice or chop food at regular intervals to form uniform pieces.

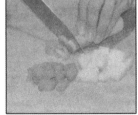

19

The Art of the KNIFE

MINCING

Rinse and dry herbs well and strip leaves from the stems. Gather herbs in a pile on the cutting board and use your guiding hand to hold them in place while you position the knife so it can slice through the pile. Once the herbs are coarsely cut, use your guiding hand fingertips to hold the tip of the knife against the cutting board. Lower the knife firmly and rapidly, repeatedly cutting through the pile of herbs or vegetables until desired fineness is achieved. Chives or scallions are minced by cutting through them repeatedly until they are sliced very fine.

SHREDDING

Tight heads of greens such as Belgian endive or cabbage can be cut in halves or quarters then chopped with a chef's knife by holding the tip of the knife in contact with the surface and making a smooth downward stroke.

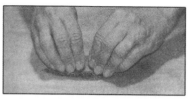

DECORATIVE SLICING

Chiffonade

The chiffonade is done by hand to cut herbs, leafy greens and other ingredients into very fine shreds that are distinct from shredding because they are much finer and uniform. Roll large loose leaves or stack small ones before cutting. Use a chef's knife to make very fine, parallel cuts to produce fine shreds.

Rondelles

Rondelles, or rounds, are easy to cut because the shape is the result of cutting a cylindrical item, such as a carrot, crosswise. Trim and peel the item as necessary and make parallel slicing cuts with a chef's knife, slicer or utility knife.

Half Moons

The basic shape can be varied by slicing the item in half to create a half moon shape.

Diagonal

The diagonal cut made by a series of parallel cuts on an angle is often used to prepare vegetables for stir fry because it exposes a greater surface for cooking.

Oblique or Roll Cut

This cut is used for long cylindrical vegetables such as parsnips, carrots and celery. The oblique cut is a shape where the cut sides are neither parallel (side by side) nor perpendicular (at right angles). Place peeled vegetable on the cutting board. Hold the knife in the same position and roll vegetable a half turn. Slice through it on the same diagonal, forming a piece with two angled edges and repeat until vegetable has been cut.

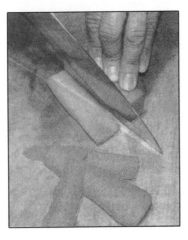

JULIENNE & BATONNET

Julienne and batonnet are long, rectangular cuts with julienne at 1/8 by 1/8 inch in thickness and 1 to 2 inches long and batonnet at 1/4 x 1/4 inch in thickness and 2 to 2-1/2 inches long. Dimensions may vary slightly, but the key to this cut is uniformity of dimension for even cooking.

Trim vegetable so that sides are straight, which makes it easier to produce even cuts (see previous page. The trimmings can be used for soups, purées or any dish where shape is not important.) Then slice the vegetable lengthwise, using parallel cuts of the proper thickness.

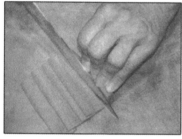

Julienne should be 1/8 inch thick

Batonnet should be 1/4 inch thick

Stack the slices, aligning the edges, and make parallel cuts of the same thickness through the stack. Cuts should be 1/8 inch apart for julienne and 1/4 inch apart for batonnet.

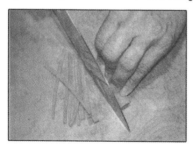

DICE

Dicing is a cutting technique that produces a cube-shaped result. First trim and peel as needed. Cut vegetable into slices of the appropriate thickness. The smallest dice is called brunoise which is derived from the french word meaning "to brown" because this cut is commonly sautéed. For a larger dice, just cut the slices to the thickness that you wish the finished dice to be. Note the dimensions on the photos below for various sized dices. The term cube refers to cuts 3/4 inch and larger. Stack slices and make even parallel cuts of the appropriate thickness. Stacking too high will produce uneven cuts. Gather sticks together and use your guiding hand to make crosswise parallel cuts through the sticks being careful cuts are all the same thickness.

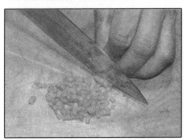

Brunoise/fine dice is 1/8 inch square from julienne cuts

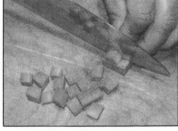

Small dice is 1/4 inch square from batonnet cuts

Medium dice is 1/3 inch square from large batonnet

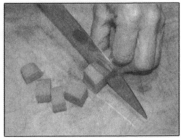

Large dice should be 3/4 inch square

ONIONS

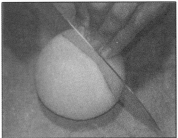

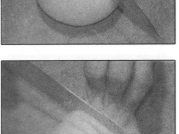

To avoid the tears that onions can bring to your eyes, use a very sharp knife so the onion will be cut, not crushed. Peel off skin and trim root end. To dice or mince onion, half the onion lengthwise through the root but leave intact.

Lay it on its side and make a series of evenly spaced, parallel, lengthwise cuts with the tip of a chef's knife again leaving the root intact.

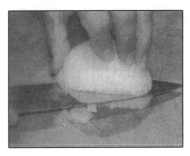

Make two or three horizontal cuts parallel to the cutting board, from the root's stem end toward the root end, but do not cut all the way through.

Make even crosswise cuts with a chef's knife all the way through from the stem to root end. The closer the cuts the finer the dice will be.

GARLIC

Garlic and onions lend the best flavor to cooking when cut by hand just before you cook them.

To prepare garlic by hand start by wrapping the entire head in a towel and press down on the top to break it into individual cloves. Press hard enough to loosen the skin on the cloves. The towel keeps the papery garlic skins from littering your work area. Use the heel of your hand or a closed fist to hit the clove.

Loosen the skin from the clove by crushing it between the flat of the blade and cutting board. Peel off the skin and remove root end of the clove.

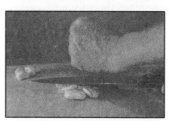

Chop cloves fairly fine with a chef's knife using a rocking motion. For a mashed garlic paste hold the knife nearly flat and mash against the cutting board.

MUSHROOMS

Clean mushrooms just before you are ready to prepare them by rinsing them quickly in cool water, just long enough to remove any dirt. Drain them and let them dry thoroughly. Some varieties need to have stems removed prior to slicing, while others can usually be left intact and just slice away the stem end to trim any dried or fibrous material.

Mushrooms can be chopped or minced, cut into slices, julienne or batonnet, or diced.

Hold the mushroom cap with your guiding hand and make slices through the cap and stem, if it has not been trimmed. To cut large amounts efficiently, slice so that slices are layered as shown in top photo.

Cut across the slices at the desired thickness.

Make crosswise cuts to mince mushrooms to even smaller size.

AVOCADOS

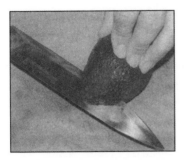

Use the fingertips of your guiding hand to control the avocado while turning the avocado against the knife blade. Again using your fingertips, twist the two halves apart.

Catch the skin of the avocado between the ball of your thumb and the flat side of a utility or paring knife blade and pull it free from the flesh.

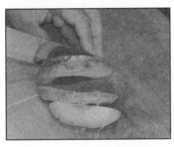

Cut the avocado into wedges. To cube avocado cut crosswise through the wedges.

As an alternate use a paring knife to dice avocado while still in the skin and use a spoon to scoop out the flesh.

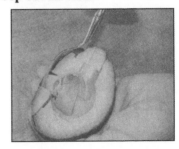

28

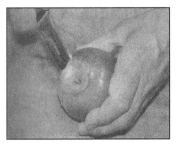

APPLES

These cutting techniques are also appropriate for fruits such as pears and vegetables such as soft-skinned squashes.

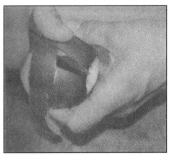

Use the tip of a paring knife to remove stem and blossom ends.

Also use the paring knife to cut away the skin. Use your guiding hand to hold and turn the apple against the blade. The peeling should be as thin as possible to avoid loss of edible fruit.

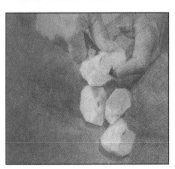

Once peeled, cut apple into quarters, and make a cut with a paring knife that scoops out the seeds.

Continue to cut the apple into wedges or slices of the desired thickness. Crosscut wedges for chopped or diced apples.

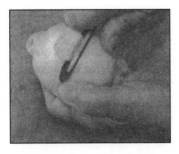

CITRUS FRUIT

Zest
Use a peeler or citrus zester to remove the brightly colored outer portion of citrus fruit peel or rind known as citrus zest. Shred or mince the zest with a chef's knife.

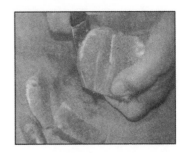

Citrus Supremes
These sections or segments are made by cutting the flesh away from the connective membranes of the fruit. First cut away both ends of the fruit. Use a chef's knife to cut skin away. Finish by cutting out each section.

The Art of the KNIFE

**SALSAS
CHUTNEYS
and SAUCES**

The Art of the KNIFE

SALSA FRESCA

Makes 1-1/2 cups.

**3 cloves garlic
1/2 serrano chili
6 plum tomatoes
6 sprigs cilantro
1 tablespoon fresh lime juice
1 tablespoon vegetable oil
Salt and pepper to taste**

Peel and mince garlic cloves and place in a medium bowl. Remove stem, membrane and seeds from the chili. Cut in small dice and add to garlic. Cut tomatoes in quarters lengthwise, remove seeds and medium dice. Add to garlic. Remove cilantro leaves from stems and mince cilantro. Add to garlic.

Toss vegetables and add the fresh lime juice, vegetable oil and salt and pepper to taste. Let stand at room temperature for at least 30 minutes and up to 2 hours before serving.

STRAWBERRY SALSA

Makes 3 cups.

**1 pint strawberries
2 tablespoons sugar
1 serrano chili
1/2 red onion
6 sprigs cilantro
3 tablespoons raspberry vinegar
Salt and pepper to taste**

Remove stems from strawberries and medium dice berries. Place in a medium bowl and toss with sugar. Cover and refrigerate for at least 1 hour and up to 2 hours.

Remove stems from chili and thinly slice across into rounds. Finely dice the red onion and add with chili to the strawberries. Remove leaves from cilantro and mince the leaves. Add to the salsa along with raspberry vinegar and salt and pepper to taste. Toss well and serve within 2 hours.

FRESH PINEAPPLE SALSA

Makes 3 cups.

**1/2 fresh pineapple
1/2 hot house cucumber
1/2 red bell pepper
1/4 red onion
1 jalapeño chili
1-inch piece fresh ginger
1 tablespoon raspberry vinegar
Salt to taste**

Peel pineapple and cut into medium dice. Cut the cucumber and red pepper into medium dice and toss with the pineapple in a medium bowl.

Finely dice the red onion and add to pineapple. Trim the end from the jalapeño, remove the membrane and seeds and finely dice. Add to pineapple. Peel the ginger and slice. Then mince the ginger. Add to pineapple along with raspberry vinegar and salt to taste. Let stand at room temperature until ready to serve and up to 2 hours.

FRESH PAPAYA SALSA

Makes 3 cups.

**1/2 red onion
1/2 red bell pepper
1/2 serrano chili
1 tablespoon vegetable oil
6 sprigs cilantro
1 large papaya
2 tablespoons fresh lime juice
Salt to taste**

Dice enough red onion to make 1/2 cup. Cut the red bell pepper into medium dice. Finely mince the serrano chili, seeds and all. Heat the oil in a small skillet and sauté the onion, red pepper and chili until wilted, about 3 minutes. Scrape into a medium bowl and cool.

Remove leaves from cilantro and mince leaves. Peel the papaya and cut in half. Scrape out the seeds and cut into a large dice. Toss cilantro and papaya with cooked vegetables. Add lime juice and salt to taste and let stand 30 minutes or refrigerate up to 3 hours.

SPICY MANGO SALSA

Makes 2 cups.

**1 large or 2 small ripe mangos
1/4 red onion
1/2 Scotch bonnet or habanero chili
3 sprigs cilantro
2 tablespoons fresh lime juice
1/4 teaspoon ground cumin
Salt and white pepper to taste**

Peel and cut mango away from the pit. Cut mango into large dice and place in a medium bowl. Dice the red onion and add to the mango.

Wearing gloves, remove seeds and membrane from chili and finely mince. Remove leaves from cilantro and mince leaves. Toss chili and cilantro with mangos. Add lime juice, cumin, salt and white pepper to taste. Let stand at room temperature 1 hour or refrigerate up to 2 hours before serving.

BLACK BEAN AND MANGO SALSA

Makes 4 cups.

2 large or 3 small ripe mangos
1/2 red onion
1 small bunch cilantro
2 serrano chilies
2 cloves garlic
2 (15-ounce) cans black beans, rinsed and
drained
3 tablespoons fresh lime juice
1 tablespoon olive oil
1 teaspoon sugar

Peel and cut mango away from the pits. Cut mangos into large dice and place in a large bowl. Dice red onion to make 3/4 cup. Remove cilantro leaves from stems and mince. Add onion and cilantro to mango.

Cut stems off serrano chili and slice across into thin slices. Peel garlic and mince and add to mangos along with chili. Toss in black beans, lime juice, olive oil and sugar. Let stand at least 30 minutes or refrigerate up to 3 hours before serving.

MEDITERRANEAN ROASTED VEGETABLE SALSA

Makes 2 cups.

**1 medium red onion, peeled
and halved crosswise
1 red bell pepper, quartered and seeded
1 zucchini, sliced
1 small eggplant, peeled and cubed
3 tablespoons olive oil
2 large tomatoes, seeded and chopped
1 tablespoon fresh lemon juice
1/2 teaspoon ground coriander
Pinch cayenne pepper
Salt to taste
1/3 cup crumbled feta cheese
Tortilla or pita chips for dipping**

Brush onion, pepper with half the olive oil and toss the zucchini and eggplant with the remaining oil. Preheat broiler and lay a sheet of aluminum foil on a baking sheet. Arrange onion, pepper, zucchini and eggplant on the foil far from heat source and broil until browned and tender. Remove vegetables broiler and coarsely chop.

Toss chopped vegetables with tomatoes, coriander, lemon juice, cayenne and salt to taste. Let stand at room temperature for 30 minutes. Top with feta cheese before serving with chips.

RED BELL PEPPER AND FRESH PEACH SALSA

Makes 2 cups.

1 large red bell pepper
3 large fresh peaches
1 small bunch fresh basil
1/2 small bunch fresh mint
1/3 cup olive oil
3 cloves garlic
1 tablespoon fresh lime juice
Salt and pepper to taste
Pinch sugar (optional)

Cut top and bottom off red bell pepper and slice down one side to open. Remove seeds and membranes and lay flat. Peel peaches and cut in half. Remove the pit from each.

Finely mince the basil to make 1/4 cup and finely mince the mint to make 2 tablespoons. Toss with olive oil. Brush the red pepper and peaches with the herb oil and grill until browned and softened a bit. Cut red pepper into fine dice and peaches into large dice and place in a medium bowl. Add the remaining herb oil.

Peel the garlic and finely mince. Add garlic to peaches along with lime juice and salt and pepper to taste. If mixture is not sweet enough add some sugar to taste. Cover and refrigerate up to 2 hours before serving.

FRESH MANGO CORN SALSA

Makes 3 cups.

3 ears fresh yellow corn
2 tablespoons olive oil
2 fresh ripe mangos
4 green onions
1/2 bunch cilantro
2 cloves garlic
1 jarred roasted red pepper
3 tablespoons fresh lime juice
Salt to taste

Set each cob of corn in the center of a dish towel and cut down the sides to remove the kernels. The towel will keep the corn from flying too far. Heat the oil in a large nonstick skillet over medium high heat and sauté the corn until it is deep golden brown, about 5 minutes. Remove corn to a large bowl and cool.

Peel and cut mangos from pits. Cut mango into large dice and toss with corn. Slice green onions and add to corn. Remove leaves from cilantro stems and mince. Peel garlic and mince and add with cilantro to corn.

Dice roasted red pepper and toss into corn with lime juice and salt to taste. Serve immediately or let stand up to 2 hours.

SMOKY CHIPOTLE
GRILLED CORN SALSA

Makes 3 cups.

4 ears yellow or white corn
1 small red onion
1 small red bell pepper
2 serrano chilies
1/2 bunch cilantro
2 canned chipotle chilies in adobo sauce
1/4 cup fresh lime juice
1/3 cup corn oil
Salt and pepper to taste

Husk the corn and grill, turning often until lightly charred. Cut kernels off corn and transfer to a medium bowl. Cut the onion and red bell pepper into medium dice and add to the corn. Cut stems off serrano chili and slice across into thin slices and add to mixture. Remove leaves from cilantro stems and mince. Mince the chipotle chilies and add to corn along with cilantro, lime juice, corn oil and salt and pepper to taste.

Let stand at room temperature at least 30 minutes or refrigerate at least 1 hour and up to 2 days. Serve at room temperature.

BLACK BEAN RELISH

Makes 2-1/2 cups.

**2 plum tomatoes
1/2 red bell pepper
1/4 red onion
1 serrano chili
1 (15-ounce) can black beans,
rinsed and drained
2 tablespoons white wine vinegar
1 tablespoon vegetable oil
Salt and pepper to taste**

Cut tomatoes lengthwise in quarters. Remove seeds. Cut tomatoes into medium dice and place in a medium bowl. Cut red bell pepper and red onion into medium dice and add to tomatoes. Remove stem from chili and thinly slice into rings. Add to tomatoes.

Toss black beans with tomato mixture and then gently toss in the vinegar, vegetable oil and salt and pepper to taste. Let stand 30 minutes at room temperature or refrigerate for up to 3 hours.

CRANBERRY PEPPER RELISH

Makes 2-1/2 cups.

2 red bell peppers
2 cups cranberries
1 medium onion
1 jalapeño chili
3/4 cup sugar
1/2 cup cider vinegar
1/4 teaspoon salt
Pinch crushed red pepper flakes

Cut the peppers into medium dice. Coarsely chop the cranberries and finely chop the onion. Cut chili in half and remove seeds and membrane. Finely mince the jalapeño and add to a medium saucepan along with bell pepper, cranberries and onions.

Add the sugar, vinegar, salt and red pepper flakes to the cranberries in the saucepan, stirring to combine. Bring mixture to a boil, then lower heat and simmer, stirring often, until mixture thickens and the cranberries soften, about 30 minutes. Cool to room temperature. Refrigerate up to 2 weeks.

The Art of the KNIFE

MANGO AND CRANBERRY RELISH

Makes 2-1/2 cups.

**2 mangos
8 ounces fresh cranberries
1/2 medium unpeeled orange
1/2 cup sugar**

Peel mango and cut off pit. Finely chop mango and place in a bowl. Finely chop the cranberries and add to the mango. Remove seeds from orange, if any, and finely chop, including the skin. Stir into mango mixture with the sugar. Let stand 1 hour before serving or relish keeps in the refrigerator for 3 days.

CURRIED CRANBERRY AND PEACH CHUTNEY

Makes 3 cups.

**1 small onion
1 (16-ounce) can sliced peaches, drained
3 slices crystallized ginger
1 (12-ounce) bag fresh or frozen cranberries
1/2 cup fresh orange juice
1/2 cup red wine vinegar
3/4 cup sugar
1/2 teaspoon curry powder
1/2 teaspoon salt
1/8 teaspoon powdered mustard
1/8 teaspoon ground ginger**

Chop onions and place in a large saucepan. Cut peaches into large dice and add to the onions. Mince the crystallized ginger and add to the pan along with the remaining ingredients.

Bring mixture to a boil and then lower heat and simmer, stirring occasionally, for 20 minutes or until all cranberries pop and mixture thickens. Cool to room temperature and then refrigerate at least 12 hours and up to 3 weeks.

CRANBERRY APRICOT CHUTNEY

Makes 3 cups.

12 ounces dried apricots
1 large red onion
3 cloves garlic
3 sprigs fresh rosemary
1 cup water
2/3 cup cider vinegar
2/3 cup golden brown sugar
3/4 cup dried cranberries
2 teaspoons grated lemon zest
1/2 teaspoon salt
Pinch crushed red pepper flakes
1/2 cup toasted slivered almonds

Chop dried apricots and place in a large saucepan. Dice the onion and add to apricots. Peel garlic and mince. Remove leaves from rosemary stems and finely dice. Add rosemary and garlic to apricots.

Add the water, vinegar, brown sugar, dried cranberries, lemon zest, salt and red pepper flakes. Bring to a boil and then lower heat and simmer until thickened, about 25 minutes. Stir in almonds and cool to room temperature. Chill at least 3 hours and up to 2 weeks.

PEAR CRANBERRY CHUTNEY

Makes 3 cups.

**2 Bosc pears
2-inch piece fresh ginger
1 small onion
1 (12-ounce) bag fresh or frozen cranberries
1/3 cup dark brown sugar
1/4 cup real maple syrup
1/2 cup raisins
2 teaspoons grated lemon zest
1/4 cup cider vinegar
1 teaspoon mustard seeds
1/2 teaspoon crushed red pepper flakes
1/4 teaspoon salt**

Peel, core and dice the pears and place in a large saucepan. Peel ginger, slice and finely dice. Add to pears. Chop the onion and add to saucepan along with all the remaining ingredients.

Bring to a boil and then lower heat and simmer, stirring occasionally, until all cranberries have popped and pears are tender, about 25 minutes. Cool to room temperature and then refrigerate 1 hour and up to 2 weeks.

PAPAYA-MANGO CHUTNEY

Makes 2-1/2 cups.

1 papaya
1 mango
1 large Granny Smith apple
1 small onion
1/2 red bell pepper
4 slices crystallized ginger
1/2 cup golden raisins
3/4 cup sugar
3/4 cup cider vinegar
1 teaspoon yellow mustard seeds
1/2 teaspoon salt
1/4 teaspoon crushed red pepper flakes

Peel papaya, cut in half and scoop out seeds. Cut into large dice. Peel mango and cut away from pit. Cut flesh into large dice. Peel and core apple and cut into large dice. Remove seeds and membrane from red bell pepper and cut into medium dice. Combine fruit and vegetables in a large saucepan.

Mince the crystallized ginger and add to the saucepan along with all the remaining ingredients. Bring to a boil and then lower heat and cook, stirring occasionally, until vegetables are cooked and mixture has a jam-like consistency. Cool to room temperature and then refrigerate up to 2 weeks.

MANGO AND DRIED CRANBERRY CHUTNEY

Makes 2 cups.

1 Granny Smith apple
1 small onion
4 slices crystallized ginger
1 (16-ounce) bag frozen mango cubes, thawed
3/4 cup dried cranberries
3/4 cup sugar
1/2 cup cider vinegar
3/4 teaspoon yellow mustard seeds
1/2 teaspoon salt
1/4 teaspoon crushed red pepper flakes

Peel and core apple and cut into large dice. Peel and chop the onion and place in a large saucepan with the apple.

Mince the crystallized ginger and add to the apple along with the thawed mango cubes and all the remaining ingredients. Bring to a boil and then lower the heat and cook, stirring occasionally, until the fruit is tender and mixture has a jam-like consistency. Cool to room temperature and then refrigerate up to 1-1/2 weeks.

PEACH CHUTNEY

Makes 2 cups.

1-1/2 pounds ripe fresh peaches
1/2 red bell pepper
1/2 medium onion
1 large jalapeño chili
4 cloves garlic
1-inch piece fresh ginger
1/2 cup golden brown sugar
1/2 cup white sugar
1/2 cup cider vinegar
1/3 cup golden raisins
1/2 teaspoon salt

Peel peaches, remove pits and cut into large dice. Place in a large saucepan. Remove seeds and membrane from red bell pepper and cut into medium dice. Chop the onion and add to peaches along with red pepper. Remove stem end from chili. Cut in half lengthwise and remove all seeds and membrane. Finely mince the chili and add to the peaches.

Peel and mince the garlic and ginger and add to the peaches. Stir in all the remaining ingredients and bring to a boil. Lower heat and simmer, stirring occasionally, until fruit and vegetables are tender and sauce reaches a jam-like consistency. Cool to room temperature and refrigerate up to 1 week.

TROPICAL FRUIT CHUTNEY

Makes 2 cups.

**1/4 fresh pineapple
1 mango
1 papaya
1 medium red onion
2 cloves garlic
1-inch piece fresh ginger
1/2 serrano chili
1 kiwi
3/4 cup red wine vinegar
1/2 cup golden brown sugar
1/2 teaspoon ground ginger
1/2 teaspoon ground cumin
1/2 teaspoon pepper
1/4 teaspoon salt**

Peel and core the pineapple and cut into large dice. Peel the mango and cut fruit from the pit. Cut into large dice. Peel papaya and cut in half. Scoop out seeds and cut into large dice. Combine fruit in a large saucepan.

Peel onion and chop. Peel and mince garlic and ginger and add to fruit along with onion. Cut stem off serrano chili and slice across into thin slices and add to mixture. Peel kiwi and cut into medium dice. Cover and set aside.

Add all the remaining ingredients except kiwi to the saucepan and bring to a boil. Lower heat and simmer, stirring occasionally, until fruit is tender and sauce reaches a jam-like consistency. Cool to room temperature, stir in kiwi and refrigerate up to 2 weeks.

TOMATO CILANTRO CHUTNEY

Makes 2 cups.

**1 bunch cilantro
1 small shallot
2 cloves garlic
1/2-inch piece fresh ginger
3 tablespoons unsalted butter
5 large plum tomatoes
1/4 cup sugar
4 teaspoons tomato paste
4 teaspoons fresh lemon juice
1/2 teaspoon salt**

Remove leaves from cilantro stems and chop the leaves. Cover and set aside. Peel and mince the shallot, garlic and ginger. Melt the butter in a medium saucepan and add the shallots, garlic and ginger. Sauté for 1 to 2 minutes to soften.

Peel tomatoes and cut in quarters lengthwise. Scoop out seeds and cut into medium dice. Add to the saucepan along with the cilantro, sugar, tomato paste, lemon juice and salt. Bring to a boil, lower heat and simmer until tomatoes are tender, about 15 minutes. Cool and use within 4 hours.

PAPAYA CHUTNEY SAUCE

Makes 2 cups.

**2 papayas
1 medium red onion
2 cloves garlic
1/2-inch piece fresh ginger
1 cup red wine vinegar
1/2 cup golden brown sugar
1/4 cup dried cranberries
1 stick cinnamon
1/2 teaspoon salt**

Peel the papayas and cut in half. Scoop out the seeds and cut into large dice. Peel and chop the onion. Peel the garlic and ginger and mince.

Combine all the ingredients in a large saucepan and bring to a boil. Lower the heat and simmer, stirring occasionally, until the onions are tender, about 15 minutes. Cool to room temperature. Remove the cinnamon stick and pureé in the food processor or blender until smooth. Sauce may be used immediately or refrigerated up to 2 weeks.

CRANAPPLE GINGER SAUCE

Makes 4 cups.

2 medium Granny Smith apples
1-1/2 inches fresh ginger
2 (12-ounce) bags fresh or frozen cranberries
1-1/2 cups sugar
1-1/2 cups water
3 tablespoons raspberry or cider vinegar
1 tablespoon grated orange zest

Peel and core apples and cut into medium dice. Peel ginger and finely mince. Combine apples with ginger and cranberries in a large saucepan. Stir in the sugar, water, vinegar and orange zest.

Bring mixture to a boil and then lower heat and simmer, stirring occasionally, until all the cranberries pop and the apples are tender, about 15 minutes. Cool and then refrigerate at least 1-1/2 hours and up to 1 week.

JALAPENO KETCHUP

Makes 2-1/2 cups.

3 tomatoes
1/2 onion
2 to 3 jalapeño chilies
2 cloves garlic
1/2 cup red wine vinegar
1/2 cup canned crushed tomatoes or
tomato sauce
1/4 cup water
1/4 cup golden brown sugar
1/2 teaspoon chili powder
2 to 3 teaspoons hot pepper sauce
Salt and pepper to taste

Peel tomatoes and cut in half crosswise. Squeeze out the seeds and cut into medium dice and place in a large saucepan. Chop the onion and add to tomatoes. Trim ends from jalapenos and cut in half lengthwise. Scoop out seeds and membrane and finely dice. Add to tomatoes. Peel and mince garlic and add to tomatoes with all the remaining ingredients.

Bring to a boil and then lower heat and simmer for 20 to 25 minutes, stirring occasionally. Remove from heat and cool slightly before pureeing in the blender or food processor. Cool completely and then chill until serving time and up to 1 week.

The Art of the KNIFE

COLA BBQ SAUCE

Makes 2 cups.

**1/2 onion
2 cloves garlic
1 cup cola
1 cup ketchup
1/4 cup Worcestershire sauce
1 teaspoon liquid smoke
1/4 cup A-1 sauce
1/2 teaspoon pepper**

Finely dice onion and place in a medium saucepan. Peel and mince garlic and add to onion.

Stir in the cola, ketchup, Worcestershire sauce, liquid smoke, A-1 sauce and pepper. Bring to a bowl over medium heat and then reduce heat and simmer gently for about 10 minutes or until boiled down by one quarter. Use immediately or cool and then refrigerate for up to 1 month.

CHUTNEY BBQ SAUCE

Makes 2-1/2 cups.

**1 medium onion
2 cloves garlic
2 tablespoons vegetable oil
1 (12-ounce) bottle ketchup-style chili sauce
1 (9 to 10 ounce) jar mango chutney or
homemade chutney of choice
1/3 cup cider vinegar
2 tablespoons Worcestershire sauce
2 tablespoons Dijon mustard
1-1/2 teaspoons hot pepper sauce**

Finely dice onion and place in a bowl. Peel and mince garlic and add to onion.

Heat oil in a medium saucepan and add onion and garlic. Sauté until tender, about 5 minutes. Stir in the chili sauce, chutney, vinegar, Worcestershire sauce and mustard. Bring to a boil over medium heat. Reduce heat and simmer about 10 minutes, stirring often, until thickened. Stir in hot pepper sauce and cool to room temperature. Use immediately or cool and refrigerate up to 3 days.

RED WINE PEACH SAUCE

Makes 2-1/2 cups.

**1-1/2-inch piece fresh ginger
1 (16-ounce) can sliced peaches, drained
1 medium onion
1 tablespoon vegetable oil
5 tablespoons sugar
1-1/2 cups dry red wine
3/4 cup soy sauce
1/4 cup balsamic vinegar
1/2 teaspoon pepper**

Peel and mince ginger. Cover and set aside. Cut peaches into medium dice. Cover and set aside.

Finely chop the onion. Heat the oil in a medium saucepan and add the onion and sugar. Cook, until onion is golden and sugar caramelizes, stirring often, about 6 minutes.

Stir in wine, soy sauce, balsamic vinegar, ginger and pepper. Bring to a boil and cook 1 minute. Remove from heat and stir in peaches.

THAI CHILI-GARLIC SAUCE

Makes 1/2 cup.

**1 green onion
4 cloves garlic
1/3 cup fish sauce
2 tablespoons water
2 tablespoons golden brown sugar
3 tablespoons fresh lime juice
2 teaspoons crushed red pepper flakes**

Finely mince green onion. Peel and mince garlic.

Combine fish sauce, water and sugar in a small saucepan. Heat over medium low heat stirring constantly, until sugar dissolves and sauce is smooth and slightly thickened.

Remove from heat and stir in lime juice, garlic, green onion and red pepper flakes. Cool to room temperature or refrigerate before using.

FRESH TOMATILLO SAUCE

Makes 2 cups.

**1 pound fresh tomatillos
4 sprigs cilantro
1 medium onion
1 jalapeño chili
1 clove garlic
1 tablespoon olive oil
Salt and pepper to taste**

Peel husks off tomatillos and rinse. Drop into a large pot of boiling water and cook until they turn olive green in color, about 5 minutes. Drain and transfer to a blender. Remove leaves from cilantro and mince. Cover and set aside.

Coarsely chop the onion. Trim stem end from chili, cut in half lengthwise and scoop out seeds. Coarsely chop. Peel and chop garlic. Add onion, chili and garlic to the blender and pureé until smooth.

Heat olive oil in a large skillet over medium heat. Add the tomatillo sauce and cook, stirring occasionally, until slightly thickened, about 5 minutes. Remove from heat and stir in the cilantro. Season to taste with salt and pepper.

SPANISH ROMESCO SAUCE

Makes 1-1/2 cups.

**6 red bell peppers
6 cloves garlic
1/3 cup slivered toasted almonds
1 tablespoon grated lemon zest
1/4 teaspoon cayenne pepper
1/2 cup extra-virgin olive oil
Salt and pepper to taste**

Cut tops and bottoms off peppers and slit down one side. Open peppers and flatten. Preheat broiler and lay a sheet of aluminum foil on a baking sheet. Arrange the peppers on the foil and broil close to the heat source for 8 to 10 minutes or until pepper skins are blackened. Wrap peppers in foil and let stand at least 10 minutes. Unwrap and peel off skins. Cut into large pieces.

Peel garlic and drop into a running food processor. Continue processing until finely chopped. Stop processor and add the roasted peppers, almonds, lemon zest and cayenne. Process until smooth.

With processor running, gradually pour in the oil. Season to taste with salt and pepper. Cover and refrigerate overnight or up to 2 days. Serve at room temperature.

GREEK TZATZIKI SAUCE

Makes 3 cups.

1 long hot house cucumber
1 teaspoon salt
3 cloves garlic
4 sprigs fresh dill
2 cups plain yogurt
1 cup sour cream
1/4 teaspoon pepper

Finely dice or grate the cucumber and place in a colander. Toss with salt and let drain for at least 1 hour. Squeeze out excess liquid from cucumber.

Peel garlic and finely mince. Remove leaves from dill and finely mince. Stir garlic and dill into yogurt and sour cream. Stir in cucumber and pepper. Chill at least 1 hour before serving. Keeps 1 day refrigerated.

SAFFRON AIOLI

Makes 1 cup.

**2 cloves garlic
1 cup mayonnaise
1/4 cup red wine vinegar
1 tablespoon honey
Large pinch saffron threads
Salt and pepper to taste**

Peel garlic and finely mince. Stir into mayonnaise, cover and refrigerate.

Place vinegar, honey and saffron in a small saucepan. Bring to a boil, stirring constantly, over medium heat. Cool completely. Stir into garlic mayonnaise and season to taste with salt and pepper.

TARRAGON TARTAR SAUCE

Makes 1-1/2 cups.

**3 green onions
1/2 bunch Italian parsley
2 small gherkin pickles
4 sprigs fresh tarragon
1 cup mayonnaise
2 tablespoons fresh lemon juice
1/4 teaspoon sweet paprika
1/2 teaspoon hot pepper sauce or to taste
Salt and pepper to taste**

Trim ends from green onions and finely chop to make 1/2 cup. Remove leaves from parsley and finely chop to make 1/4 cup. Cut pickles into small dice to make 1/4 cup. Remove leaves from tarragon stems and finely mince.

Place mayonnaise in a medium bowl and stir in all chopped ingredients as well as the lemon juice, paprika and hot sauce to taste. Season to taste with salt and pepper. Cover and refrigerate up to 24 hours.

SWEET PEPPER AIOLI

Makes 1 cup .

**1 large red bell pepper
2 cloves garlic
1 green onion
1/2 cup mayonnaise
2 tablespoons mango or peach chutney
1 tablespoon fresh lemon juice
1/8 teaspoon cayenne pepper
Salt and pepper to taste**

Cut tops and bottoms off pepper and slit down one side. Open pepper and flatten. Preheat broiler and lay a sheet of aluminum foil on a baking sheet. Lay the pepper on the foil and broil close to the heat source for 8 to 10 minutes or until pepper skins are blackened. Wrap pepper in foil and let stand at least 10 minutes. Unwrap and peel off skins. Cut the pepper into small dice.

Peel and mince garlic. Trim ends from green onion and finely chop. Stir diced peppers, garlic and green onion into mayonnaise along with chutney, lemon juice and cayenne. Season to taste with salt and pepper. Cover and refrigerate at least 1 hour and up to 24 hours.

CHIPOTLE REMOULADE

Makes 1-1/4 cups.

2 cloves garlic
1 green onion
3 sprigs cilantro
1 canned chipotle chili in adobo sauce
1 cup mayonnaise
**2 tablespoons frozen orange juice concentrate,
thawed**

Peel and mince garlic. Trim ends from green onion and finely chop. Remove leaves from cilantro stems and mince. Finely mince the chipotle chili to make 1 teaspoon.

Place the mayonnaise in a small bowl and stir in the orange juice concentrate. Stir in the garlic, green onion, cilantro and chipotle chili. Season to taste with salt and pepper. Cover and refrigerate until just before serving.

PACIFIC RIM PESTO

Makes 1 cup.

**3 cloves garlic
2 serrano chilies
1 bunch cilantro
1/2 bunch fresh mint
1/3 cup toasted macadamia nuts
1/2 teaspoon salt
2 tablespoons fresh lemon juice
1/2 cup vegetable oil**

Peel garlic and coarsely chop. Trim ends from serrano chilies and slice. Cut top of cilantro from stems. You should have a packed cup of cilantro. Remove leaves from mint stems and coarsely chop.

Place garlic, chilies, cilantro, mint, macadamia nuts and salt in food processor. Pulse to chop and combine. With processor running, add the lemon juice and vegetable oil to make a paste.

SUN-DRIED TOMATO
BEURRE BLANC

Makes 1 cup.

3 large basil leaves
3 sun-dried tomato halves, packed in oil
1 medium shallot
2 tablespoons fresh lemon juice
1/4 cup dry white wine
1/4 cup heavy whipping cream
1/2 cup unsalted butter, diced and chilled
Salt and pepper to taste

Stack basil leaves and cut across into strips. Turn strips the other direction and slice again to form small dice. Set aside. Pat the tomatoes dry and then cut into small dice. Set aside.

Peel and finely dice the shallot. Place shallot in a small saucepan. Add the lemon juice and wine and bring to a boil. Cook to reduce by 2/3. Add cream and sun-dried tomatoes and return to simmer. Remove from heat and add the butter a piece at a time, allowing once piece to dissolve before adding the next. Stir in the basil and season to taste with salt and pepper.

CHILI HOLLANDAISE

Makes 1 cup.

**1 or 2 serrano chilies
3 sprigs cilantro
3 large egg yolks
1-1/2 tablespoons fresh lemon juice
1/2 cup unsalted butter, melted
Salt and pepper to taste**

Cut stem ends off chilies and slice in half lengthwise. Scoop out seeds and membranes and finely mince. Remove leaves from cilantro stems and finely mince.

Whisk the eggs yolks and lemon juice into the top of a double boiler and set over simmering water. Whisking constantly, slowly add the hot melted butter. As the sauce thickens you may add the butter faster. When all the butter has been added and the sauce is thick and creamy, remove from heat and stir in the chilies and cilantro. Season to taste with salt and pepper. Serve immediately or place in a thermos to keep warm for several hours.

The Art of the KNIFE

CHIMICHURRI SAUCE

Makes 1 cup.

1 bunch fresh Italian parsley
2 sprigs fresh oregano
2 cloves garlic
1 large carrot
1/2 small onion
1/4 cup chicken broth
2 tablespoons extra virgin olive oil
2 tablespoons white wine vinegar
1/4 teaspoon salt
fresh gound pepper to taste

Remove leaves from parsley stems to make 1 cup packed. Coarsely chop the parsley. Remove leaves from oregano and coarsely chop. Peel and coarsely chop garlic. Peel the carrots and cut into julienne strips. Cut the onion into brunoise (see page 24) dice.

Combine the parsley, broth, olive oil, vinegar, oregano, salt, pepper and garlic in the blender or food processor and process until smooth. Pour into a bowl; stir in carrot and onion. Set aside for at least 1 hour.

FRESH BASIL FETA SAUCE

Makes 1 cup.

**4 large fresh basil leaves
2/3 cup heavy whipping cream
1 tablespoon Balsamic vinegar
1 teaspoon Dijon mustard
4 ounces sheep's milk feta cheese, crumbled**

Stack basil leaves on top of each other and slice across into thin julienne strips (see page 22). Turn and cut across into small dice. Set aside.

Whisk cream, vinegar and mustard together in a small saucepan. Bring to a simmer. Stir in the basil and feta cheese and continue to cook over medium heat, stirring constantly, until sauce is heated through, 1 minute longer.

ROASTED GARLIC PORT SAUCE

Makes 2 cups.

**1 large head garlic
1 tablespoon olive oil
4 cups chicken broth, divided use
1 medium shallot
3 tablespoons unsalted butter, divided use
1/2 cup port wine
Salt and pepper to taste**

Slice top off garlic to expose the cloves. Lay the garlic on a sheet of heavy-duty aluminum foil and drizzle with olive oil. Wrap garlic in foil and roast at 400 degrees for 1 hour. Cool slightly and then squeeze the garlic out into a blender. Add 1/2 cup chicken broth and pureé.

Peel and finely chop the shallot. Melt 1 tablespoon butter in a 3 quart saucepan over medium high heat. Add the shallot and toss until tender, about 2 minutes. Add the port and bring to a boil, scraping up any browned bits from the bottom of the pan. Cook until only 2 tablespoons port remain.

Add the garlic broth mixture and the remaining chicken broth to the saucepan and bring to a boil. Cook until liquid is reduced by half. Remove from heat and whisk in the remaining 2 tablespoons butter. Season to taste with salt and pepper.

CREOLE SAUCE

Makes 2 cups.

**1/4 small onion
1 stalk celery
1/4 medium green bell pepper
1-1/2 cups diced seeded plum tomatoes
6 sprigs Italian parsley
3 tablespoons unsalted butter
1-1/2 teaspoons Cajun/Creole seasoning
1 teaspoon sugar
1/2 teaspoon dried oregano
1/4 teaspoon dried thyme
1/4 cup dry vermouth
2 teaspoons Louisiana Hot Sauce
1/4 cup chicken broth
1/2 cup heavy cream**

Cut onion, celery and bell pepper into small dice. Cut tomatoes lengthwise into quarters and remove seeds. Cut tomatoes into medium dice. Remove leaves from parsley stems and finely chop.

Melt butter in a large skillet over medium high heat. Add the onion, celery and bell pepper and sauté until tender, about 5 minutes. Add the Cajun/Creole seasoning, sugar, oregano, thyme and tomatoes. Toss for 2 minutes or until the tomatoes soften slightly. Stir in the vermouth and bring to a simmer.

Stir in the hot sauce, broth and cream and return to a simmer. Cook for 3 minutes or until sauce reduces and thickens slightly. Stir in parsley.

QUICK MUSTARD SAUCE

Makes 1 cup.

2 small shallots
6 sprigs Italian parsley
1/2 cup dry vermouth
1 cup heavy whipping cream
2 tablespoons Dijon mustard
Salt and pepper to taste

Peel and finely chop the shallots. Remove leaves from parsley stems and finely chop the leaves.

Place shallots in a medium saucepan with wine. Bring to a boil and cook until most liquid evaporates, about 4 minutes.

Add the whipping cream and bring to a simmer. Cook until sauce is reduced slightly, about 2 minutes. Whisk in the mustard and simmer for 2 minutes longer to blend flavors. Season to taste with salt and pepper and stir in parsley.

CABERNET SHALLOT SAUCE

Makes 1-3/4 cups.

**3/4 pound shallots
6 cloves garlic
8 sprigs fresh thyme
2 sprigs fresh rosemary
2 tablespoons olive oil
1 teaspoon sugar
1 tablespoon flour
1 bay leaf
Pinch ground nutmeg
3 cups beef broth
1-1/2 cups Cabernet Sauvignon wine
1/4 cup brandy
Salt and pepper to taste**

Peel and slice the shallots. Peel and mince the garlic. Remove leaves from thyme and rosemary stalks.

Heat olive oil in a large saucepan over medium heat. Add shallots and garlic and sprinkle with sugar. Cook until shallots are tender and golden in color, about 20 minutes.

Stir in flour, bay leaf, thyme, rosemary and nutmeg and toss for 1 minute. Add the broth, wine and brandy. Bring to a boil and cook until reduced to 1-3/4 cups, about 20 minutes. Remove bay leaf and season to taste with salt and pepper.

SHIITAKE MUSHROOM SAUCE

Makes 2 cups.

**3 cloves garlic
1 large shallot
8 ounces fresh shiitake mushrooms
3 sprigs fresh thyme
2 tablespoons unsalted butter
1/2 cup dry white wine or vermouth
3/4 cup chicken broth
1 cup heavy whipping cream
Salt and pepper to taste**

Peel and finely chop garlic. Peel and finely dice shallot. Remove stems from mushrooms and wipe clean with a damp paper towel. Cut mushrooms across into thin slices. Remove leaves from thyme stems.

Melt butter in a large skillet over medium high heat. Add the garlic and shallots and cook until tender, about 3 minutes. Stir in the mushrooms and thyme and cook until mushrooms give off their liquid and then liquid evaporates, about 7 minutes.

Stir in wine and cook until absorbed, scraping up the browned bits from the bottom of the pan. Add the chicken broth and cream and bring to a boil. Boil until sauce reduces to desired consistency, about 4 minutes. Season to taste with salt and pepper.

CHARDONNAY MUSTARD SAUCE

Makes 1 cup.

1 large shallot
6 sprigs Italian parsley
1/2 cup Chardonnay wine
1 cup heavy whipping cream
2 tablespoons Dijon mustard
Salt and pepper to taste

Peel shallot and finely chop. Remove leaves from parsley stems and mince.

Place shallots and Chardonnay in a medium saucepan over medium high heat. Bring to a boil and cook until wine is reduced to 1 tablespoon, about 4 minutes.

Add the cream and lower the heat to medium. Whisk in the mustard and simmer until thickened and reduced enough to coat the back of a spoon, 3 to 4 minutes. Stir in parsley and season to taste with salt and pepper.

KAHLUA CHOCOLATE SAUCE

Makes 1 cup.

6 ounces good quality semisweet chocolate
1/4 cup light corn syrup
3/4 cup heavy whipping cream
2 tablespoons Kahlua

Finely chop the chocolate by placing the block of chocolate on a cutting board. With a chef's knife shave the chocolate into small pieces, starting at one corner. When the cutting surface gets too wide, move to another corner and continue until all the chocolate is chopped.

In a medium saucepan combine the corn syrup and whipping cream. Bring to a full boil. Remove from heat and stir in the chocolate until completely melted. Stir in the Kahlua. Serve sauce immediately or reheat later.

MEXICAN CHOCOLATE SAUCE

Makes 1 cup.

**6 ounces good quality semisweet chocolate
1/4 cup light corn syrup
3/4 cup heavy whipping cream
1/2 teaspoon ground cinnamon
1/2 teaspoon vanilla**

Finely chop the chocolate by placing the block of chocolate on a cutting board. With a chef's knife shave the chocolate into small pieces, starting at one corner. When the cutting surface gets too wide, move to another corner and continue until all the chocolate is chopped.

In a medium saucepan combine the corn syrup, whipping cream and cinnamon. Bring to a full boil. Remove from heat and stir in the chocolate until completely melted. Stir in the vanilla. Serve sauce immediately or reheat later.

The Art of the KNIFE

The Art of the KNIFE

APPETIZERS

CROSTINI WITH BASIL, MOZZARELLA AND TOMATOES

Makes 20.

**3 cloves garlic
1/2 cup olive oil
4 large plum tomatoes
8 to 10 fresh basil leaves
1 crusty baguette
1 pound fresh mozzarella cheese
1/2 cup toasted pine nuts**

Peel and mince garlic. Stir garlic into olive oil and let rest at room temperature for at least 15 minutes and up to 2 hours.

Cut tomatoes in quarters lengthwise and remove seeds. Dice tomatoes. Stack the basil leaves and dice.

Preheat oven to 400 degrees. Slice baguette on a diagonal into 20 slices, each about 1/2-inch thick. Arrange bread slices on a baking sheet and brush one side with the garlic oil. Bake for 7 to 9 minutes or until lightly toasted.

Preheat broiler. Drain mozzarella cheese and cut into 10 thin slices; cut slices in half to make 20 pieces. Arrange a slice of cheese on each piece of bread. Broil just until cheese softens – it won't melt like regular mozzarella. Top Crostini with tomatoes, basil and pine nuts and serve.

BRUCHETTA WITH GORGONZOLA AND ROASTED RED PEPPERS

Makes 12.

7 cloves garlic
1/2 cup olive oil
1 roasted red bell pepper
1/2 teaspoon salt
1 teaspoon olive oil
12 pitted Kalamata olives
8 chives
1 crusty loaf Italian or French bread
6 ounces Gorgonzola cheese, crumbled
8 ounces cream cheese, softened

Peel and mince garlic and stir 6 cloves into the olive oil. Let rest at room temperature for at least 15 minutes and up to 2 hours. Cut roasted pepper into 12 batonnet strips (see page 22). Toss with remaining clove minced garlic, salt and olive oil. Cut olives into slivers and mince the chives.

Heat grill, indoors or out. Slice bread diagonally into 12 slices, each about 1-inch thick. Brush both sides with the garlic oil and grill each side, about 2 minutes or until golden brown. Transfer bread to a platter.

Combine Gorgonzola and cream cheese and spread on the grilled bread. Arrange red peppers and olives on top and sprinkle with chives.

The Art of the KNIFE

ROASTED GARLIC AND CAMBOZOLA CHEESE TOASTS

Makes 24.

**6 large heads roasted garlic
3 tablespoons olive oil
8 fresh basil leaves
1 cup drained sun-dried tomatoes in oil
1 tablespoon balsamic vinegar
1/2 teaspoon freshly ground pepper
1 crusty baguette
8 to 12 ounces Cambozola cheese,
at room temperature**

Preheat oven to 400 degrees. Slice off top of each head of garlic to expose the cloves and place in a pie plate. Drizzle with olive oil and cover tightly with aluminum foil. Bake for 1 hour or until garlic is golden brown. Cool.

Dice sun-dried tomatoes and toss with balsamic vinegar and pepper; set aside. Stack the basil leaves and cut across into julienne strips. Squeeze garlic from bulbs and mash.

Slice baguette diagonally into 24 slices, 1/2-inch thick. Arrange on a baking sheet and bake to lightly toast for 8 minutes. Spread garlic on baguette toasts and top with a piece of Cambozola, the sun-dried tomatoes and a bit of basil.

SWISS CHEESE SHRIMP TOASTS

Makes 20.

**1 handful fresh parsley
3 sprigs fresh thyme
2 tablespoons melted butter
10 thin slices white bread
6 ounces cooked small shrimp
1/2 cup shredded Swiss cheese
1/3 cup mayonnaise
1 teaspoon paprika**

Wash and dry the parsley and thyme. Finely mince both. Stir thyme into melted butter.

Preheat oven to 400 degrees. Using a 2 inch round biscuit cutter, cut 2 circles from each bread slice. Chop enough of the scraps of bread to make 1/2 cup. Brush bread rounds with thyme butter and arrange on a baking sheet. Bake for 8 minutes or until golden.

Chop the shrimp and combine with the chopped bread, Swiss cheese and mayonnaise to make a paste. Spread shrimp on toast rounds and sprinkle with paprika. Broil briefly until bubbly. Sprinkle with parsley.

The Art of the **KNIFE**

SALSA RANCH DIP WITH HOMEMADE TORTILLA CHIPS

Serves 8.

**4 sprigs fresh cilantro
1 (1-ounce) package Ranch Dip Mix
16 ounces sour cream
1/2 cup thick and chunky salsa
Tortilla chips for serving
Baby Carrots and Celery Sticks for serving**

Remove cilantro leaves from stems and mince. Set aside for garnish. Prepare vegetables for serving.

In a medium bowl stir the dip mix into the sour cream. Stir in the salsa. Cover and refrigerate at least 1 hour. Keeps up to 4 days. Serve dip sprinkled with cilantro and surrounded with tortilla chips, carrots and celery.

CREAMY CHILI DIP

Serves 8 to 10.

**3 green onions
1 (8-ounce) package cream cheese, softened
1 (15-ounce) can chili without beans
1 (4-ounce) can diced green chilies
Fritos or Tortilla Chips for serving**

Trim ends from green onions and chop. Cut cream cheese into cubes. Combine cream cheese, chili, diced chilies and green onions in a 1-1/2 quart casserole or deep pie plate and cook in the microwave oven on 50 % power for 8 to 10 minutes, stirring every 2 minutes. Keep warm in a chafing dish, on a hot plate or in a Fondue pot and serve with chips for dipping.

The Art of the KNIFE

GUACAMOLE

Makes 2 cups.

2 large ripe avocados
1 tomato
1/2 serrano chili
1 clove garlic
2 sprigs fresh cilantro
1 tablespoon fresh lime juice
Salt to taste

Peel avocados and cut into medium dice. Place in a strainer and rinse in cold water to retard color change. Transfer to a bowl and mash.

Cut tomato in half crosswise and squeeze out the seeds. Remove the stem and cut into small dice. Finely mince the chili to make 1/2 teaspoon. Peel and mince the garlic. Remove cilantro leaves and mince. Add tomato, chili, garlic and cilantro to avocados along with lime juice and salt to taste.

CREAMY AVOCADO DIP

Makes 1-1/2 cups.

2 large avocados
1 clove garlic
1/3 cup sour cream
1 teaspoon seasoned salt

Peel avocados and cut into medium dice. Place in a strainer and rinse in cold water to retard color change. Transfer to a bowl and mash.

Peel garlic and mince. Add garlic, sour cream and seasoned salt to avocados and stir to combine well.

The Art of the KNIFE

GOAT CHEESE AND PISTACHIO SPREAD WITH TUSCANY TOASTS

Makes 24.

1 bunch chives
1/3 cup toasted salted pistachio nuts
7 cloves garlic
1/2 cup olive oil
1 crusty baguette
1/2 cup freshly grated Parmesan cheese
11 ounces soft goat cheese
1/2 cup unsalted butter, softened

Chop enough chives to make 1/4 cup. Cut a few more into 1-inch lengths for garnish. Set aside. Chop the pistachios and set aside.

Preheat oven to 400 degrees. Peel garlic and mince. Stir 6 cloves garlic into the olive oil and let stand for at least 15 minutes and up to 2 hours. Slice the baguette diagonally into 24 slices, 1/2-inch thick. Brush with garlic oil and sprinkle with Parmesan. Bake for 8 minutes or until golden brown.

Mash the goat cheese and butter together in a medium bowl. Stir in the remaining clove minced garlic, the minced chives and the chopped pistachios. Transfer to a serving bowl. Cover and refrigerate several hours or overnight. Garnish with chives and serve with toasts for spreading.

ROASTED RED BELL PEPPER AND FETA DIP

Makes 2 cups.

**3 large red bell peppers
3 sprigs fresh oregano
1/2 cup crumbled feta cheese
2 tablespoons extra-virgin olive oil
Pinch cayenne pepper
Salt and pepper to taste
4 pita breads, cut into wedges or crackers**

Preheat broiler. Cut the top and bottom off the peppers and then slice down one side and open peppers flat; remove all the seeds. Place peppers on a foil-lined baking sheet under the broiler. Broil 8 to 10 minutes or until blackened. Remove and wrap peppers in foil for 10 minutes to steam. Peel off skins and chop.

Remove oregano leaves from stems and mince leaves to make 1 tablespoon.

Place peppers, feta cheese, olive oil and cayenne in the food processor; pulse to coarsely chop. Add the oregano and pulse to mix in. Season to taste with salt and pepper. Transfer to a bowl, cover and refrigerate for at least one hour and up to 2 days. Serve as a spread for pita wedges or crackers.

HOT ARTICHOKE DILL DIP

Makes 2-1/2 cups.

2 cloves garlic
3 stalks fresh dill
2 slices white or French bread
2 teaspoons olive oil
1 (9-ounce) box frozen artichoke hearts, thawed
2 tablespoons butter
3/4 cup mayonnaise
1-1/2 cups shredded havarti or muenster cheese
3/4 cup freshly grated Parmesan cheese
1 crusty baguette

Peel and mince garlic and place in a medium bowl. Remove dill from stems and mince. Add to the garlic. Finely chop the bread into small dice and toss with the olive oil to make the topping. Set aside.

Coarsely chop the thawed artichoke hearts and sauté in the butter in a small skillet over medium high heat. Add to the garlic and dill. Stir in the mayonnaise and both cheeses.

Preheat the oven to 325 degrees. Transfer the artichoke dip to a pie plate and sprinkle with breadcrumbs. Bake for 30 minutes or until top is browned and dip is hot. Slice baguette and serve with dip for spreading.

BRIE CHEESE TRUFFLES

Makes 18.

1-1/2 cups toasted walnuts
1/4 red onion
4 sprigs fresh Italian parsley
3 ounces cream cheese, softened
Salt and pepper to taste
12 ounces ripe Brie cheese

Finely chop the walnuts and place in a shallow bowl.

Finely dice the onion and place in a medium bowl. Remove the leaves from the parsley stems and mince. Add to the onion. Add the cream cheese and some salt and pepper to taste. Mix together to blend thoroughly.

Using the cheese knife, cut off the rind from the Brie and cut into 18 pieces. Flatten each piece of Brie into a circle and place 1 teaspoon of the cream cheese mixture in the center of each. Gently enclose the filling with the Brie and roll into a ball.

Roll the cheese balls in the walnuts and place in candy papers. These refrigerate for 24 hours but remove from refrigerator 30 minutes before serving.

GREEK SAGANAKI

Serves 6.

**12 pitted Kalamata olives
2 lemons
1-1/2 pounds Greek Kefalotyri or Italian
Fontinella cheese
2 cups water
1 cup flour
3/4 cup olive oil
1/2 teaspoon dried oregano
1/4 teaspoon freshly ground pepper**

Cut olives into slivers and set aside. Juice one lemon and cut the second lemon into 6 wedges. Using the cheese knife, cut the cheese into 1/2-inch thick slices.

Place cheese slices in water. Place flour on a plate and heat olive oil in a large nonstick skillet until hot.

Remove cheese from water and dredge in flour. Add to oil and fry in a single layer until golden and crusty, turning with a fork, about 1 to 2 minutes per side. The cheese should be soft but not melting.

Transfer cheese to a platter and drizzle with lemon juice. Sprinkle with oregano and pepper and serve with lemon wedges.

CURRIED CHUTNEY CHEESE MOLD

Serves 8 to 10.

**1 bunch green onions
1 cup dried cranberries
1 cup toasted cashew nuts
3/4 cup bottled mango chutney
2 (8-ounce) packages cream cheese, softened
1 cup cottage cheese
1 teaspoon curry powder
1/2 cup flaked coconut
1/4 cup toasted flaked coconut
Crackers and Apple slices**

Chop enough green onions to make 1 cup. Place in a bowl. Chop the cranberries and cashew nuts and add to the green onions.

Chop the mango pieces in the chutney if large and place in a food processor. Add the cream cheese, cottage cheese and curry powder and process until smooth. Stir into the green onions mixture along with the 1/2 cup coconut.

Place mixture into a plastic wrap lined mold or bowl; cover and refrigerate for 4 hours or overnight.

To serve, unmold onto a platter and sprinkle on the toasted coconut. Surround with crackers and apples.

The Art of the KNIFE

CRAB IMPERIAL STUFFED MUSHROOMS

Makes 24.

1/4 yellow bell pepper
1/4 red onion
1 stalk celery
1 green onion
2 cloves garlic
2 sprigs fresh parsley
1 sprig fresh dill
1 tablespoon butter
1 cup mayonnaise
1 tablespoon Dijon mustard
1 teaspoon fresh lemon juice
1/2 teaspoon hot pepper sauce
1/2 teaspoon Worcestershire sauce
Salt and cayenne pepper to taste
1 pound lump crabmeat
24 large (2 to 3 inches diameter) mushrooms
1/4 cup olive oil
1/2 cup freshly grated Parmesan cheese

Cut pepper into medium dice. Cut red onion and celery into medium dice. Slice green onion. Peel and mince garlic. Mince enough parsley to make 1 tablespoon and mince enough dill to make 1 teaspoon. Melt butter in a small skillet and sauté the bell pepper, onion and celery for 2 minutes. Add the green onion and garlic and toss 30 seconds more. Cool.

In a medium bowl stir together the mayonnaise, mustard, lemon juice, hot sauce, Worcestershire sauce, salt and cayenne to taste. Stir in the cooled vegetables, the parsley and dill. Gently fold in the crabmeat.

Preheat oven to 350 degrees. Remove stems from mushrooms and wipe caps clean with a damp paper towel. Brush mushroom caps with olive oil and arrange in a baking dish. Fill mushrooms with crab mixture, mounding above the top. Sprinkle with Parmesan cheese and bake for 15 to 20 minutes or until tender and bubbly.

SUN-DRIED TOMATO PESTO STUFFED NEW POTATOES

Makes 24.

**12 small red new potatoes, uniform in size
1 teaspoon salt
1/2 cup pitted Kalamata olives
1/2 cup drained sun-dried tomatoes in oil
1/2 cup roasted red peppers
2 tablespoons capers, rinsed and drained
3 fresh basil leaves
3 fresh oregano sprigs
1 clove garlic
1 tablespoon red wine vinegar
1 tablespoon extra-virgin olive oil
1/4 teaspoon crushed red pepper flakes
24 parsley leaves for garnish**

Cut a very thin slice off the top and bottom of each potato. Cut the potatoes in half crosswise. Place in a large pot and cover with cold water. Bring to a boil and add salt. Reduce heat and simmer until tender when pierced, 10 to 15 minutes. Drain and cool.

Finely dice the olives, sun-dried tomatoes and roasted peppers. Place in a medium bowl. Mince the capers and add to the bowl. Stack the basil leaves and mince. Remove the leaves from the oregano stems and mince enough to make 1 tablespoon. Add to bowl along with basil.

Peel and mince garlic and toss into bowl along with vinegar, olive oil and red pepper flakes. Stir to combine well.

Scoop out the center of each potato half with a spoon or melon baller and fill with sun-dried tomato pesto. Top each with a parsley leaf and serve at room temperature.

ITALIAN MUSHROOM AND PROSCIUTTO TURNOVERS

Makes 30.

**2 medium onions
2 small red bell peppers
1-1/2 pounds crimini mushrooms
1 bunch Italian parsley
6 ounces prosciutto slices
6 tablespoons unsalted butter
1/3 cup dry marsala
3 tablespoons fine dry breadcrumbs
1 package frozen puff pastry sheets, thawed
1 egg whisked with 1 teaspoon water**

Finely chop the onions. Cut peppers in half and pull out seeds and membrane. Cut into strips and then across into medium dice. Trim mushroom stems and wipe mushrooms clean with damp paper towels. Slice mushrooms and finely dice. Mince parsley and then chop prosciutto.

Melt butter in a large skillet over medium high heat. Add the onions and cook 5 minutes. Stir in mushrooms and bell pepper and cook, stirring often, until mushrooms are tender and all liquid has cooked off. Add the prosciutto and Marsala and cook, stirring until liquid is evaporated. Remove to a bowl and stir in parsley and breadcrumbs. Season with salt and pepper to taste and cool completely.

Preheat oven to 400 degrees. Line two baking sheets with parchment paper.

On a lightly floured work surface roll out the puff pastry to a 15 x 9 inch rectangle. Cut each sheet into 3 strips across and 5 strips down to make 30 total squares.

Preheat oven to 400 degrees. Lightly brush two adjacent sides with the egg wash. Spoon 2 teaspoons mushroom filling onto square and fold in half to form a triangle. Press to seal edges and then crimp with a fork. Poke the top of each with the fork as well.

Transfer turnovers to baking sheets and brush with egg wash. Bake for 15 to 18 minutes or until golden brown. Serve warm.

CRAB AND MUSHROOM MINI-CHEESECAKES

Makes 24.

**1 small shallot
1/4 red bell pepper
6 white mushrooms
1 small bunch chives
1 tablespoon olive oil
1 sheet frozen puff pastry, thawed
1/2 cup crab meat
4 ounces cream cheese, softened
1/8 teaspoon powdered mustard
1/2 teaspoon salt
2 eggs, whisked
1/2 cup shredded smoked Gouda cheese**

Mince the shallot to make 1 tablespoon. Mince enough red bell pepper to make 1 tablespoon. Trim stems from mushrooms, wipe clean with a damp paper towel and then finely dice the mushrooms to make 1/2 cup. Mince chives and set aside.

Heat olive oil in a medium nonstick skillet over medium heat. Add shallot and red pepper and sauté 1 minute. Add the mushrooms and cook until all liquid evaporates and mushrooms begin to brown. Season to taste with salt and pepper and cool completely.

Preheat oven to 400 degrees. Spray 24 mini-muffin cups with nonstick spray. On a lightly floured work surface roll out the puff pastry sheet to a 12 x 14 inch rectangle. Using a 2-1/2-inch biscuit cutter, cut out 24 rounds and press into the muffin cups.

Spoon 1 teaspoon crabmeat into each cup. Mix together the cream cheese, dry mustard and salt until smooth. Beat in eggs and then fold in cooled mushroom mixture and chopped chives. Spoon egg mixture over crab. Top with a sprinkle of Gouda cheese. Bake 10 to 14 minutes or until puffed and golden. Remove and serve warm.

BACON WRAPPED SCALLOPS

Makes 16.

**1 clove garlic
1 large jalapeño chili
6 tablespoons fresh lime juice
1/4 cup vegetable oil
16 large sea scallops
8 slices bacon, cut in half crosswise**

Peel and mince garlic and place in a medium bowl. Cut jalapeño in half lengthwise and scoop out the seeds and membrane. Finely dice the chili and add to the garlic. Whisk in the lime juice and oil. Remove foot (connective tissue) from side of each scallop and add to marinade. Cover and refrigerate 1 to 2 hours.

Remove scallops from marinade and wrap outside edge with bacon. Secure with toothpicks. Broil until bacon is crispy and scallop is just done, 3 to 4 minutes per side.

SESAME SHRIMP WITH GINGER CHILI DIP

Serves 8.

**4 sprigs cilantro
4 cloves garlic
2 tablespoons rice vinegar
2 tablespoons Asian sesame oil
2 tablespoons soy sauce
1-1/2 pounds extra-large raw shrimp**

**Chili Dipping Sauce:
1-inch piece ginger root
2 tablespoons chili paste with garlic
1 tablespoon rice vinegar
1 tablespoon sugar
1 teaspoon Asian sesame oil
3/4 cup mayonnaise**

Mince cilantro and set aside. Peel and mince garlic and combine with rice vinegar, sesame oil and soy sauce. Add shrimp and toss to coat. Refrigerate covered for 2 hours. Grill shrimp 3 to 4 minutes per side.

Peel and slice and then mince ginger. Stir into chili paste, rice vinegar, sugar and sesame oil. Whisk in mayonnaise. Cover and refrigerate until serving time and up to 24 hours.

Pile grilled shrimp on a platter around a bowl of the Chili Dipping Sauce. Sprinkle with cilantro.

The Art of the KNIFE

SHRIMP SALSA DIP

Makes 2 cups.

**3 sprigs fresh cilantro
3 cloves garlic
1/2 small onion
6 plum tomatoes
1 (7-ounce) jar roasted red peppers
1/2 pound cooked medium shrimp
1 (4-ounce) can diced green chilies
2 tablespoons fresh lime juice
2 tablespoons rice vinegar
1/3 cup vegetable oil
2 teaspoons ground cumin
1 teaspoon chili powder
Salt and pepper to taste
1 bag tortilla chips**

Remove leaves from cilantro stems and mince. Place in a small bowl and set aside. Peel and mince garlic and chop onion to make 1/3 cup. Place garlic and onion in a medium bowl. Quarter tomatoes and remove seeds. Slice lengthwise and then into batonnet dice. Add to onions. Pat roasted peppers dry with paper towels and dice. Coarsely chop the shrimp and add to onions along with peppers and chilies.

Add the lime juice, rice vinegar, oil, cumin and chili powder to the cilantro and combine well. Season to taste with salt and pepper and stir into the shrimp. Serve with chips for dipping.

CILANTRO PESTO MARINATED GRILLED SHRIMP SKEWERS

Serves 8.

2 cloves garlic
2 serrano chilies
1 bunch cilantro
1 bunch Italian parsley
3 tablespoons pine nuts
3 tablespoons freshly grated parmesan cheese
1/2 teaspoon salt
1/2 cup vegetable oil
1/2 cup sour cream
1 pound extra-large shrimp, cleaned

Peel and mince garlic. Slice serrano chilies. Remove leaves from cilantro to make 1 cup. Coarsely chop parsley to make 1/2 cup.

In food processor place the garlic, chilies, cilantro, parsley, pine nuts, parmesan cheese and salt. Pulse to chop. With machine running, pour in the oil to make a paste. Remove 3 tablespoons pesto to a small bowl and stir in sour cream.

Toss shrimp with pesto, cover and refrigerate 2 hours. Thread shrimp on skewers and grill for 3 minutes per side. Remove from skewers and serve with pesto sour cream for dipping.

The Art of the KNIFE

LIME-ORANGE MARINATED GRILLED SHRIMP

Serves 8.

3 cloves garlic
1 bunch cilantro
1/2 cup fresh lime juice
1/4 cup orange marmalade
1/4 cup olive oil
1 tablespoon soy sauce
1/2 teaspoon crushed red pepper flakes
1 pound extra-large shrimp, cleaned

Peel garlic and mince. Remove leaves from cilantro stems and mince to make 1/2 cup. Stir garlic and cilantro into lime juice, marmalade, olive oil and soy sauce in a large bowl. Remove 1/3 cup to a small bowl and set aside.

Add shrimp to marinade in large bowl. Cover and refrigerate for 2 hours. Thread shrimp on skewers and grill for 4 minutes per side or until cooked through. Remove shrimp to a platter and drizzle with reserved marinade.

GRILLED AHI TUNA BITES WITH GREEN OLIVE RELISH

Serves 4.

**3 cloves garlic
1 bunch Italian parsley
3/4 cup pitted green olives
1 pound fresh ahi tuna
8 tablespoons extra-virgin olive oil
Zest of 1 lemon
3 tablespoons fresh lemon juice
1 tablespoon white wine vinegar**

Peel and mince garlic. Place half the garlic in a large bowl and half in a medium bowl. Mince the parsley leaves to make 1/2 cup and add to the medium bowl. Finely chop the green olives and add to the parsley along with 6 tablespoons olive oil, lemon juice and vinegar.

Peel the zest from the lemon with a vegetable peeler or zesting tool (see page 30) and cut into julienne strips. Add to the large bowl.

Cut the tuna into 3/4 inch cubes and add to the large bowl with the lemon zest strips. Add remaining 2 tablespoons olive oil, salt and pepper to taste. Cover and refrigerate 2 hours. Thread tuna on skewers and grill 5 to 6 minutes, turning twice. Toss with olive relish and serve.

The Art of the KNIFE

The Art of the KNIFE

SALADS AND SIDE DISHES

The Art of the KNIFE

CAESAR BLUE CHEESE SALAD

Serves 6.

**6 large white button mushrooms
1 large head romaine lettuce
6 slices bacon, cooked and crumbled
1/2 cup crumbled blue cheese
1/4 cup toasted pine nuts**

**Dressing:
2 cloves garlic, peeled
1/2 cup freshly grated Parmesan cheese
1/4 cup fresh lemon juice
1 teaspoon Worcestershire sauce
3/4 cup extra-virgin olive oil**

Wipe mushrooms clean with a damp paper towel and thinly slice. Coarsely chop lettuce and place in a salad bowl. Toss with mushrooms, bacon, blue cheese and pine nuts.

For dressing: Combine all ingredients in the food processor and blend until smooth. Season to taste with salt and pepper. Cover and refrigerate until serving time and up to 24 hours. Toss with salad and combine well.

SHRIMP PASTA CAESAR SALAD WITH TOMATOES

Serves 4.

**3 green onions
1 small bunch fresh basil
1 cup grape or other tiny tomatoes
1 medium head Romaine lettuce
1 pound extra-large shrimp,
shelled, deveined and cooked
3 cups cooked bow-tie pasta**

**Dressing:
1/2 cup freshly grated Parmesan cheese
1/4 cup fresh lemon juice
2 cloves garlic, peeled
1/2 cup extra-virgin olive oil
1/4 cup mayonnaise
1 teaspoon Worcestershire sauce**

Trim ends from green onions and slice. Stack basil leaves and slice across into julienne strips. Cut the tomatoes in half. Cut lettuce across in 1-inch thick slices. Toss these all with shrimp and pasta in a large salad bowl.

For dressing: Combine all ingredients in the food processor and blend until smooth. Season to taste with salt and pepper. Cover and refrigerate until serving time and up to 24 hours. Toss with salad and combine well.

SWEET CORN, JICAMA AND BABY SPINACH SALAD

Serves 6.

6 ears raw yellow corn
1/2 jicama
1 large red bell pepper
2 (6-ounce) bags baby spinach
3 tablespoons toasted pine nuts

Tequila Lime Dressing:
1/4 cup fresh lime juice
2 tablespoons Tequila
2 tablespoons honey
1 teaspoon white wine vinegar
1/2 cup vegetable oil
1/2 teaspoon ground cumin
Pinch cayenne pepper
Salt and pepper to taste

Remove husk and silk from corn. Stand corn upright in the center of a dish towel and cutting down the sides remove the corn kernels. Peel jicama and cut in julienne strips to make 2 cups. Remove seeds and membrane from pepper and cut in small dice. Toss all with spinach in a salad bowl.

For dressing, whisk lime juice, Tequila, honey and vinegar in a medium bowl. Whisk in the vegetable oil. Add the cumin, cayenne and salt and pepper to taste. Toss with salad and serve immediately.

STRAWBERRY AND SPINACH SALAD WITH ALMONDS

Serves 8.

2 baskets fresh strawberries
3 (6-ounce) bags baby spinach
3 tablespoons toasted sesame seeds
3 tablespoons slivered almonds

Dressing:
2 green onions
6 tablespoons vegetable oil
3 tablespoons raspberry vinegar
4 tablespoons sugar
1 teaspoon Worcestershire sauce
1/8 teaspoon hot pepper sauce

Remove stems from strawberries and slice across into thin slices. Toss spinach with sesame seeds and almonds.

For dressing, finely mince the green onions. Whisk together the oil, vinegar and sugar until sugar dissolves. Stir in green onions, Worcestershire and hot sauce. Season to taste with salt and pepper. Cover and chill until serving time and up to 24 hours.

Add strawberries and dressing to spinach and toss well but gently. Serve immediately.

MIXED GREENS AND CUCUMBER SALAD WITH GORGONZOLA

Serves 6 to 8.

**1 small cucumber
1 bunch radishes
2 tomatoes
2 (6-ounce) bags mixed baby greens
2 ounces Gorgonzola cheese, crumbled**

**Dressing:
2 small shallots
3 cloves garlic
1/4 cup red wine vinegar
2 tablespoons Dijon mustard
4 ounces gorgonzola cheese, crumbled
3/4 cup extra-virgin olive oil**

Peel and scrape out seeds from cucumber. Thinly slice across into half moon shapes. Slice radishes. Cut tomatoes into wedges. Toss lettuce with cucumbers, radishes and tomatoes in a salad bowl.

For dressing, quarter shallots. Peel garlic. Mix both together in the food processor Add the vinegar, mustard and 4 ounces gorgonzola. Pureé until smooth. Add the olive oil and process until smooth. Season with salt and pepper.

Toss salad with about 1/2 cup dressing or as needed. Serve topped with remaining gorgonzola.

ROASTED RED POTATO SALAD WITH DILL DRESSING

Serves 6.

1 red bell pepper, diced
1-1/2 pounds whole tiny new potatoes,
halved or quartered
1 shallot
1 tablespoon chopped fresh dill
1 tablespoon olive oil
1 tablespoon fresh lemon juice

Dill Dressing:
1/4 cup chopped fresh dill
3 tablespoons mayonnaise
3 tablespoons sour cream
1 tablespoon lemon juice
1 teaspoon lemon zest

Cut bell pepper into medium dice and set aside. Cut potatoes in half or quarters. Mince shallot and chop dill for potatoes and dressing. Place potatoes in a large bowl. Toss with olive oil, shallot, lemon juice and dill. Arrange on a baking sheet in a single layer and roast at 425 degrees for 25 to 35 minutes or until tender.

In a small bowl whisk together all the dressing ingredients. Toss with warm potatoes and red pepper. Serve warm or cover and chill up to 24 hours.

COUSCOUS SALAD WITH GRILLED VEGETABLES AND BASIL LEMON CAPER VINAIGRETTE

Serves 6.

1 eggplant
2 medium zucchini
3 large leeks
1 large red bell pepper, cut in half
4 sprigs fresh thyme
1 sprig fresh rosemary
2 tablespoons olive oil
1 tablespoon balsamic vinegar
2-1/2 cups water
1 teaspoon salt
1 (10 ounce) box couscous
1 cup Kalamata olives, pitted and halved

Vinaigrette:
1/4 cup olive oil
6 tablespoons fresh lemon juice
3 tablespoons capers, rinsed
6 fresh basil leaves

Peel eggplant and cut lengthwise into six wedges. Trim ends from zucchini and cut in half lengthwise. Trim off top and bottom of leeks and slice in half lengthwise. Cut bell pepper in half. Cut olives in half lengthwise. Stack basil leaves and slice across into julienne strips. Set aside for dressing.

Stir together the olive oil, balsamic, thyme and rosemary. Toss with vegetables and grill until tender, about 15 minutes, turning often. Remove to a cutting board and let cool.

Bring water to a boil and stir in the salt and couscous. Remove from heat, cover and let stand until water is absorbed, about 5 minutes. Fluff couscous with fork. Transfer to a large bowl.

For dressing, whisk together the olive oil, lemon juice, capers and basil. Cut roasted vegetables into 3/4-inch pieces and toss with couscous. Add vinaigrette and olives and toss well. Season with salt and pepper to taste. Let stand 30 minutes at room temperature before serving. You may also add 1 cup cooked baby shrimp to the couscous.

MEXICAN COLE SLAW WITH SALSA DRESSING

Serves 8.

**1 medium head green cabbage
1 red bell pepper
1/2 small red onion
1 bunch cilantro
1 cup frozen corn, thawed
1/2 cup mayonnaise
1/3 cup sour cream
1/3 cup medium salsa
1 tablespoon red wine vinegar
1/2 teaspoon ground cumin**

Cut cabbage in half and remove the core. Cut into thin fine shreds. Cut the red pepper into medium dice. Finely chop red onion to make 1/2 cup. Remove cilantro leaves and finely chop. Toss cabbage, pepper, red onion, cilantro and corn in a large bowl.

In a medium bowl whisk together the mayonnaise, sour cream, salsa, vinegar and cumin. Season to taste with salt and pepper. Up to 2 hours before serving, toss the dressing with the slaw adding only enough dressing to coat well. Cover and chill until serving time.

CALIFORNIA COLE SLAW

Serves 6.

1 medium head green cabbage
1 large carrot
1/2 cup mayonnaise
1/2 cup sour cream
3 tablespoons white wine vinegar
3 tablespoons sugar
1 teaspoon salt
1/4 teaspoon freshly ground pepper

Cut cabbage in half and remove the core. Cut into thin fine shreds. Peel carrot and cut into julienne strips.

In a large bowl whisk together the mayonnaise, sour cream, vinegar, sugar, salt and pepper. Toss in the cabbage and carrot to coat well. Cover and refrigerate up to 6 hours.

ROASTED EGGPLANT STEAKS TOPPED WITH GARBANZO BEAN AND ROASTED PEPPER SALAD

Serves 6.

**1 (1-1/2 pound) eggplant
2 roasted red bell peppers
1/2 cup pitted Kalamata olives
1 small bunch fresh oregano
6 cloves garlic
1 (15 ounce) can garbanzo beans,
rinsed and drained
4 ounces feta cheese, crumbled
1/4 cup balsamic vinegar
4 teaspoons soy sauce
1/2 cup olive oil**

Peel eggplant and slice lengthwise into six (1/2-inch thick) slices. Peel roasted peppers and cut into medium dice. Cut olives in half lengthwise. Remove oregano leaves and mince. Peel and mince garlic.

In a large bowl toss roasted peppers with garbanzos, olives, feta and oregano. Whisk together balsamic vinegar, garlic and soy sauce. Gradually whisk in olive oil. Season with salt and pepper.

Brush eggplant slices with some of the dressing and grill, 4 to 5 minutes per side. Toss remaining dressing into salad and spoon over eggplant steaks to serve.

TOFU AND VEGETABLE SLAW

Makes 2 cups.

**8 ounces baked Teriyaki tofu
1 small head romaine lettuce
1/4 head Napa cabbage
1 small carrot
1 small red bell pepper
2 green onions**

**Creamy Curry Dressing:
2 cloves garlic
1-inch piece fresh ginger root
1 teaspoon vegetable oil
1/2 cup heavy whipping cream
2 tablespoons white wine vinegar
2 tablespoons mango chutney
1 teaspoon curry powder
Pinch crushed red pepper flakes**

Cut tofu into batonnet strips (see page 22). Cut lettuce and cabbage across into thin strips. Peel carrot and cut into julienne strips. Cut red pepper into julienne strips. Cut green onions on a diagonal into thin strips. Combine all in a large bowl.

For dressing: Peel garlic and ginger and mince. Heat oil in a small nonstick skillet and sauté the garlic and ginger. Whisk in the cream, vinegar, chutney, curry powder and pepper flakes with the garlic-ginger mixture and toss with salad.

BLACK BEAN AND RED PEPPER SALAD

Serves 4 to 6.

**2 large red bell peppers
1 yellow bell pepper
1 small red onion
1/2 bunch Italian parsley
6 leaves fresh basil
2 cloves garlic
1 (15-ounce) can black beans,
rinsed and drained
1-1/2 tablespoons red wine vinegar
1 tablespoon olive oil
1 teaspoon grated orange zest**

Remove seeds and membranes from peppers and cut into medium dice. Chop enough onion to make 1/2 cup. Remove parsley leaves and chop. Stack basil leaves and chop. Peel and mince garlic.

Combine the peppers, onion, parsley, basil, garlic and beans in a medium bowl. Add the vinegar, oil and orange zest, tossing well. Season to taste with salt and pepper and let stand 30 minutes at room temperature or refrigerate up to 4 hours.

PASTA SALAD WITH ROASTED SUMMER VEGETABLES AND FETA

Serves 4 to 6.

**1 medium zucchini
1 small eggplant, peeled
1 red onion
1 yellow bell pepper
2 tomatoes
3 cloves garlic
4 sprigs fresh oregano
1/2 cup olive oil
1/2 pound bow-tie pasta, cooked, drained and rinsed in cold water
3 tablespoons balsamic vinegar
Salt and pepper to taste
1/2 cup crumbled feta cheese**

Trim ends from zucchini and cut in half lengthwise. Cut eggplant in half lengthwise. Peel onion and cut in half crosswise. Cut yellow pepper in sections and remove seeds and membrane. Cut tomatoes in half crosswise and squeeze out seeds. Coarsely chop.

Peel garlic and mince. Remove leaves from oregano stems and mince. Stir together the olive oil, garlic and oregano. Brush some of the oil on all the vegetables except the tomatoes and grill for 5 to 6 minutes per side or until very tender. Remove to a cutting board and let cool. Coarsely chop vegetables and add to pasta with the remaining oil mixture, balsamic vinegar, tomatoes and feta cheese. Toss well.

MANDARIN ORANGE AND JICAMA SALAD

Serves 6.

**1 small jicama
3 green onions
2 (11-ounce) cans Mandarin Oranges, drained
8 lettuces leaves**

**Dressing:
1/3 cup vegetable oil
1/4 cup white wine vinegar
3 tablespoons honey
1 teaspoon ground cumin
1 teaspoon chili powder
Salt and pepper to taste**

Peel jicama and slice into 1/4-inch thick slices. Cut slices across into medium julienne. Slice green onions. Toss jicama with green onions and mandarin oranges in a large bowl. Cover and chill.

To make the dressing, whisk together the oil, vinegar, honey, cumin and chili powder. Season to taste with salt and pepper. Just before serving toss dressing into salad. Serve on lettuce leaves.

APPLE AND CRANBERRY WALDORF SALAD

Serves 6.

**3 Granny Smith green apples
3 stalks celery
1 cup walnuts, toasted
1/2 cup dried cranberries
6 butter lettuce leaves**

**Dressing:
1/2 cup mayonnaise
1/2 cup applesauce
3 tablespoons honey
1 tablespoon fresh lemon juice**

Core but do not peel apples and cut into bite size chunks. Cut celery into medium dice. Coarsely chop the toasted walnuts.

Stir all the dressing ingredients together and toss with apple, celery, walnuts and dried cranberries shortly before serving. Spoon onto lettuce leaves to serve.

MELON FRUIT SALAD WITH LIME YOGURT SAUCE

Serves 8.

**1/2 cantaloupe
1/2 honeydew melon
1/2 fresh pineapple
1 papaya
1 cup strawberries
2 cups seedless red grapes
1/2 cup plain yogurt
1/4 cup honey
1/4 cup fresh lime juice
1 teaspoon grated lime zest**

Wash the outside of the cantaloupe, seed and peel. Cut into 1-inch cubes. Seed, peel and cube the honeydew melon. Peel, core and cube the pineapple. Peel papaya, scoop out seeds and cut into cubes. Slice strawberries in half. Remove grapes from stems. Combine fruit in a large bowl.

For sauce, whisk together yogurt, honey, lime juice and zest. Cover and chill until 15 minutes before serving time. Toss yogurt with fruit and let stand a few minutes before serving.

JICAMA AND ORANGE CUCUMBER SALAD

Serves 8.

1/2 jicama
1 red bell pepper
1/2 hot house cucumber
2 green onions
2 oranges
4 sprigs cilantro
1/4 cup olive oil
2 tablespoons fresh lime juice
1/2 teaspoon salt
Cayenne pepper to taste

Peel jicama and cut into medium dice to make 2 cups. Cut red pepper and cucumber into medium dice. Slice green onions. Peel and section oranges (see page 30) and then chop into medium dice. Remove cilantro leaves and mince.

Toss jicama, red pepper, cucumber, green onions and oranges in a large bowl. Whisk together the olive oil, lime juice, cilantro, salt and cayenne to taste. Stir dressing into salad and chill, covered, at least 1 hour but no longer than 8 hours.

CUCUMBER SALAD

Makes 2 cups.

**1 hot house cucumber
1 red or green chili (optional)
1/2 cup vinegar
1/2 cup water
1/2 cup sugar
1 teaspoon salt**

Very thinly slice the cucumber and place in a medium bowl. If using the chili, remove seeds and membrane and finely dice. Toss with cucumbers.

Combine vinegar, water, sugar and salt in a small saucepan. Bring to a boil, stirring constantly to dissolve the sugar. Pour hot liquid over the cucumber and let cool. Cover and refrigerate up to 2 days.

BLACK BEAN, RICE AND CORN SALAD

Serves 6.

**2 ears yellow corn
1 red bell pepper
1 yellow or orange bell pepper
4 green onions
2 cloves garlic
1/2 cup olive oil
1/4 cup cider vinegar
1 tablespoon Dijon mustard
1 teaspoon ground cumin
1-1/2 cups cooked long-grain white rice, cooled
1 (15-ounce) can black beans,
rinsed and drained**

Set corn on a dish towel and cut off kernels. Transfer corn to a large bowl. Cut red and yellow or orange peppers into medium dice. Slice green onions. Toss peppers and green onions with corn. Toss in the rice and beans.

Peel and mince the garlic. Whisk oil, vinegar, mustard, cumin and garlic in small bowl. Toss dressing with rice mixture and season to taste with salt and pepper. Cover and refrigerate up to 6 hours.

The Art of the KNIFE

RICE, ASPARAGUS AND CUCUMBER SALAD

Serves 4 to 6.

1/2 pound asparagus
1/3 hot house cucumber
2 green onions
6 sprigs fresh dill
1-1/4 cups cooked long-grain white rice, cooled
1 tablespoon Dijon mustard
1-1/2 teaspoons sugar
1-1/2 teaspoons white wine vinegar
1-1/2 tablespoons vegetable oil

Trim asparagus and cut into 1-inch lengths. Cook asparagus with 2 tablespoons water in a covered dish on HIGH power in the microwave for 2 minutes. Drain and rinse in cold water; Drain well. Place in a medium bowl.

Dice the cucumber to make 3/4 cup. Slice green onions and add to asparagus along with cucumber and rice.

Remove dill leaves from stems and place in a small bowl. Add the mustard, sugar, vinegar and oil. Stir to combine well. Toss with rice, cover and refrigerate up to 2 hours.

.

PROSCIUTTO WRAPPED ASPARAGUS WITH BLUE CHEESE

Serves 8.

32 asparagus spears
3 fresh basil leaves
1/2 cup balsamic vinegar
1/2 cup vegetable oil
1/2 cup olive oil
1/2 teaspoon salt
1/2 teaspoon freshly ground pepper
1/2 teaspoon fresh lemon juice
32 slices prosciutto, 4 inches long
4 ounces blue cheese, crumbled
8 butter lettuce leaves

Trim asparagus to 4 inch lengths. Cook asparagus with 2 tablespoons water in a covered dish on HIGH power in the microwave for 2 to 3 minutes. Drain and rinse in cold water; Drain well.

Stack basil leaves and mince. Combine with vinegar, oils, salt, pepper and lemon juice in a small bowl, whisking to combine.

Wrap each asparagus spear in a slice of prosciutto. Arrange 4 wrapped asparagus on each lettuce leaf and top with blue cheese. Drizzle with dressing.

PESTO PASTA SALAD

Serves 8.

**1 large red bell pepper, roasted
1 (15-ounce) can ripe black olives
1 pound fusilli pasta, cooked, drained and
rinsed in cold water to cool
1/3 cup pine nuts, toasted
3/4 cup prepared basil pesto sauce
1 cup or more mayonnaise**

Cut roasted pepper into julienne strips (see page 22). Cut the olives into slivers lengthwise. Toss with cooled pasta and pine nuts.

Stir pesto into 1 cup mayonnaise and stir into pasta. Cover and refrigerate until serving time, up to 6 hours. Add more mayonnaise if salad seems dry.

CHICKEN AND PASTA SALAD

Serves 8.

2 red bell peppers
4 stalks celery
1 red onion
1 (12-ounce) jar pitted Kalamata olives
1 bunch fresh dill
1 large cooked rotisserie chicken
1 pound penne, cooked and rinsed
in cold water to cool
3 tablespoons white wine vinegar
1 tablespoon lemon juice
2 tablespoons mayonnaise
2 tablespoons Dijon mustard
2/3 cup olive oil

Cut the red peppers into medium dice. Cut the celery into medium dice. Chop the red onion. Drain the olives and cut into slivers lengthwise. Remove dill leaves and mince. Remove chicken from bones and cut into medium dice.

In a large bowl toss together the pasta, peppers, celery, onion, olives, dill and chicken. For dressing, whisk together the vinegar, lemon juice, mayonnaise, mustard and salt and pepper to taste. Slowly whisk in the olive oil. Add the dressing to salad and toss well.

BLUE CHEESE POTATO SALAD

Serves 8.

3 pounds small red potatoes
3 green onions
3 stalks celery
1/4 cup dry white wine
3/4 cup mayonnaise
3/4 cup sour cream
1-1/2 tablespoons cider vinegar
1-1/2 tablespoons Dijon mustard
1/4 pound blue cheese, crumbled

Quarter potatoes or cut into 1-inch cubes. Place in a large pot and cover with cold water. Bring to a boil, adding 2 teaspoons of salt when water boils. Simmer until potatoes are tender, about 10 minutes longer. Drain and transfer to a bowl. Add wine and season with salt and pepper. Cool completely.

Slice the green onions and cut the celery into small dice. Add to potatoes along with remaining ingredients. Mix well. Cover and refrigerate up to 24 hours.

POTATO SALAD WITH CREAMY ORANGE DRESSING

Serves 10.

**5 pounds russet potatoes
1 onion
1 cup sweet gherkin pickles
1 (8-ounce) bottle French dressing
(the orange kind)
4 hard boiled eggs
1 to 2 cups mayonnaise
Salt and pepper**

Peel potatoes and cut into 1-inch cubes. Place potatoes in a large pot and cover with cold water. Bring water to a boil, adding 2 teaspoons salt as water boils. Simmer until potatoes are tender, about 10 minutes longer. Drain and transfer to a large bowl.

Chop the onion and cut the pickles into medium dice. Add to the hot potatoes along with the French dressing, tossing to coat well. Let stand or chill until cold – up to overnight.

Shortly before serving, slice the hard-boiled eggs and add to the salad with enough mayonnaise to make a creamy dressing. Season to taste with salt and pepper. Refrigerate until serving time and up to 24 hours longer.

ARTICHOKE, POTATO AND RED PEPPER SALAD

Serves 4.

1 pound small white potatoes
1 (6-ounce) jar marinated artichoke hearts,
undrained
2 red bell peppers, roasted
2 green onions
4 tablespoons fresh lemon juice

Slice potatoes and place in a medium pot of cold water. Bring water to a boil adding 1 teaspoon salt to water as it boils. Simmer potatoes until tender, about 10 minutes. Drain and transfer to a medium bowl. Drain artichoke hearts, reserving liquid. Dice artichoke hearts and toss with hot potatoes. Add lemon juice and cool to room temperature.

Cut roasted peppers into julienne strips. Slice green onions. Add to potato salad and season to taste with salt and pepper. Serve immediately or chill, but bring to room temperature before serving.

CHIPOTLE POTATO SALAD WITH CORN AND RED ONION

Serves 8.

**3 pounds red potatoes
1 medium red onion
2 pickled jalapeños
2 tablespoons pickled jalapeño juice
3 stalks celery
1 large ear yellow corn
3 hard-boiled eggs
6 sprigs cilantro
1 tablespoon chipotle chilies in adobo
1 cup mayonnaise
1 tablespoon fresh lime juice**

Cut the potatoes into 1-inch cubes and place in a large pot of cold water. Bring water to a boil adding 1 teaspoon salt to water as it boils. Simmer potatoes until tender, about 10 minutes. Drain and transfer to a large bowl. Chop red onion and pickled jalapeños and add to potatoes along with juice. Cool.

Cut celery into medium dice. Set corn on a dish towel and cut off kernels. Coarsely chop the eggs. Remove cilantro leaves from stems and mince.

Stir celery, corn and eggs into potatoes and salt to taste. Stir together the mayonnaise with chipotle chilies, cilantro and lime juice. Toss with potatoes and chill until ready to serve and up to 6 hours.

ROASTED POBLANO AND RED PEPPER POTATO SALAD

Serves 6 to 8.

**2 medium fresh poblano (pasilla) chilies, roasted
1 red bell pepper, roasted
2 ears fresh corn
6 plum tomatoes
3 green onions
8 sprigs cilantro
1 jalapeño chili
1-1/2 pounds small red potatoes
2 cloves garlic, peeled
2 tablespoons fresh lemon juice
2 tablespoons olive oil**

Peel poblaño chilies and red pepper and cut into medium dice. Place the corn on a dish towel and cut off the kernels. Cut the tomatoes into quarters lengthwise. Scoop out the seeds, slice lengthwise and then across to dice. Slice the green onions. Remove the cilantro leaves and mince. Remove the seeds and membrane from jalapeño and mince to make 1 teaspoon. Peel and mince garlic.

Cut potatoes in half and then into 1/4 inch thick slices. Place potatoes in a large pot and cover with cold water. Bring to a boil, adding 1 teaspoon salt to water as it boils. Simmer until tender, about 5 minutes. Drain and chill in a large bowl. Mix chilies, peppers, corn, tomatoes, green onions, cilantro, jalapeño and garlic with potatoes. Add lemon juice and olive oil and season with salt and pepper.

ITALIAN CHOPPED SALAD

Serves 6.

1 medium red onion
2 tablespoons white wine vinegar
1 large head romaine lettuce
1 red bell pepper
1 fresh fennel bulb
8 ounces pitted kalamata olives
2 ounces thinly sliced Italian dry salami
1 (15-ounce) can garbanzo beans, rinsed and drained
1/2 cup feta cheese, crumbled

Dressing:
6 tablespoons extra-virgin olive oil
3 tablespoons white wine vinegar
1 teaspoon dried oregano
1 clove garlic, minced

Thinly slice the onion and place in a small bowl. Cover with water and stir in the vinegar. Let stand at least 10 minutes and then drain well. Coarsely chop the lettuce. Cut the red pepper and fennel into medium dice. Slice the olives. Stack the salami slices and cut into julienne strips.

For dressing, whisk all ingredients in a small bowl. Season to taste with salt and pepper.

Combine all salad ingredients in a large bowl and toss with dressing. Serve immediately.

The Art of the KNIFE

CHICKEN CHOPPED SALAD WITH PEPPERONI AND OLIVES

Serves 6.

Dressing:
2 cloves garlic
2/3 cup olive oil
1/3 cup red wine vinegar
1 tablespoon Dijon mustard

4 skinless boneless chicken breast halves
1 large head romaine lettuce
8 plum tomatoes
1 large ear yellow corn
3/4 cup pitted Kalamata olives
6 fresh basil leaves
6 sprigs Italian parsley
2 ounces sliced pepperoni

Peel garlic and mince. Whisk with olive oil, vinegar and mustard to make the dressing. Season to taste with salt and pepper. Trim chicken breasts and pound between two sheets of plastic wrap to an even 1/2-inch thickness. Pour 1/4 cup dressing over chicken and let stand 30 minutes. Grill chicken 4 minutes per side. Cool and cut into large dice.

Coarsely chop lettuce and transfer to a large bowl. Cut tomatoes into 4 wedges and scoop out the seeds. Cut into medium dice. Place corn on a dish towel and cut off kernels. Chop olives, basil and parsley. Cut the pepperoni into medium dice and toss all with lettuce and remaining dressing.

GREEK CHOPPED SALAD WITH SHRIMP

Serves 6.

1 large head romaine lettuce
1 red bell pepper
1 medium red onion
1 medium fennel bulb
1/4 cup pitted Kalamata olives
1/2 pound cooked medium shrimp

Dressing:
3 sprigs fresh oregano
1 clove garlic
6 tablespoons olive oil
3 tablespoons white wine vinegar

Coarsely chop the lettuce and place in a large bowl. Cut the red pepper, red onion and fennel into medium dice and add to lettuce. Coarsely chop the olives and shrimp and add to lettuce.

For dressing, remove oregano leaves from stems and chop to make 1 tablespoon. Peel and mince garlic and combine with oregano, olive oil and vinegar. Season to taste with salt and pepper and toss with salad. Serve immediately.

CHICKEN, BLACK BEAN AND GOAT CHEESE TOSTADA SALADS

Serves 6.

Beans:
1 medium red onion
2 jalapeño chilies
2 tablespoons vegetable oil
1 teaspoon chili powder
1/2 teaspoon ground cumin
2 (15-ounce) cans black beans,
rinsed and drained
2 tablespoons fresh lime juice

Chicken:
4 boneless skinless chicken breast halves
2 tablespoons vegetable oil
1-1/2 teaspoons chili powder
3/4 teaspoon ground cumin

Salad:
1 small head romaine lettuce
3/4 cup cilantro leaves
1/4 cup vegetable oil
1 tablespoon fresh lime juice

Tostadas:
6 small flour tortillas
1/2 cup vegetable oil
8 ounces soft goat cheese, crumbled
1/2 cup purchased salsa
6 fresh cilantro sprigs

For beans, chop onion. Trim stem ends off chilies and scoop out seeds and membrane. Finely dice. Sauté the onion and chilies in oil in a medium saucepan over medium heat until tender, about 8 minutes. Add chili powder and cumin and then beans and lime juice. Cook until heated through, stirring and mashing beans slightly with a spoon, about 4 minutes.

For chicken, trim and cut into large dice. Heat vegetable oil in a medium nonstick skillet over medium high heat. Toss chicken with chili powder, cumin, salt and pepper and add to skillet. Toss until cooked through. Remove from heat.

For salad, cut lettuce across into thin shreds. Just before serving toss lettuce with cilantro, oil and lime juice. Season to taste with salt and pepper.

Cut tortillas in half and then crosswise into 1-inch strips. Fry tortillas strips in oil until crisp. Drain well on paper towels.

To assemble, arrange tortillas on six plates. Spoon beans over and top with goat cheese. Mound salad on top and then chicken, salsa and a sprig of cilantro for each.

CHOPPED ROMAINE SALAD WITH THOUSAND ISLAND DRESSING

Serves 4.

**1/4 roasted red pepper
1 hard-boiled egg
1/2 small dill pickle
1 green onion
2/3 cup mayonnaise
1/4 cup ketchup style chili sauce
1 tablespoon Dijon mustard
1 tablespoon capers, drained and rinsed
Tabasco to taste
1 medium head romaine lettuce
12 tiny cherry or grape tomatoes**

Cut roasted pepper into small dice. Finely chop egg and pickle and green onion. Toss all with mayonnaise, chili sauce, mustard and capers. Season to taste with salt, pepper and Tabasco. Dressing keeps 2 days in refrigerator.

Coarsely chop lettuce and place in a medium salad bowl. Set aside. When ready to serve toss with dressing and top with tomatoes.

CHOPPED SALAD WITH SMOKY CILANTRO DRESSING

Serves 4 to 6.

Dressing:
1/2 bunch cilantro
2 cloves garlic
1 chipotle chili in adobo
3 green onions
1/4 cup fresh lime juice
1 teaspoon Dijon mustard
2 teaspoons sugar
1/2 teaspoon salt
1/2 cup vegetable oil

Salad:
1 small head romaine
1/4 head green cabbage
1 roasted red pepper
1/4 medium jicama
3/4 cup frozen corn, thawed
1/2 cup crumbled feta cheese
1 cup crushed blue corn tortilla chips

For dressing, remove cilantro leaves from stems. Peel garlic and cut in half. Mince chipotle and green onions. Place cilantro, garlic, chipotle, lime juice, mustard, sugar and salt in blender and pureé. Whisk in oil and green onions.

Coarsely chop romaine, cabbage, pepper and jicama. Toss together with corn and dressing. Top with cheese and chips and serve immediately.

CHOPPED SALAD WITH SALSA VERDE DRESSING

Serves 4.

Dressing:
4 tomatillos
1/2 bunch cilantro
1/2 jalapeño chili
2 cloves garlic
3 green onions
6 tablespoons fresh lime juice
1/2 cup vegetable oil

Salad:
1 small head romaine
1/4 head green cabbage
3 plum tomatoes
1/4 medium jicama
1 avocado
3/4 cup frozen corn, thawed
1/2 pound cooked medium shrimp
1/2 cup crumbled feta cheese
1 cup crushed blue corn tortilla chips

Remove husks from tomatillos and rinse. Cut into quarters. Remove cilantro leaves and seeds from jalapeño. Peel garlic and chop green onions. Place all in blender with lime juice and pureé. Whisk in oil. Coarsely chop lettuce and cabbage and place in a salad bowl. Quarter tomatoes and scoop out seeds. Peel and cut jicama into medium dice. Peel and cut avocado into medium dice. Chop shrimp. Toss all together with dressing and serve.

GRILLED SALMON AND CORN RELISH SALAD

Serves 4.

Basil Vinaigrette: 1 bunch fresh basil
3 sprigs fresh tarragon
4 cloves garlic
1/3 cup balsamic vinegar
1/3 cup red wine vinegar
2 teaspoons chili paste with garlic
1/2 cup olive oil

Salmon: 4 (6-ounce) skinless salmon fillets
1 (6-ounce) bag mixed baby greens
2 large tomatoes

Relish: 4 ears yellow corn
1/4 green bell pepper
1/4 red bell pepper
1/2 small red onion
1 (4-ounce) can sliced black olives

For vinaigrette, stack basil leaves and chop. Remove tarragon leaves from stems and mince. Peel garlic and mince. Stir all together with vinegar, chili paste and olive oil. Pour 3/4 cup over salmon and marinate 1 hour. Grill 4 to 5 minutes per side. Slice tomatoes.

For relish, cut corn from cobs and cut peppers and onion into small dice. Toss with corn, olives and 1/3 cup vinaigrette. Place greens and tomatoes on plates and top with salmon and corn relish. Drizzle all with dressing.

CHICKEN SALAD WITH HOISIN DRESSING AND WON TON CRISPS

Serves 4 to 5.

20 won ton squares
2 cups vegetable oil
1 medium head romaine lettuce
3 green onions
1 small red bell pepper
1 small cucumber, peeled and seeded
1 roasted chicken
1/3 cup roasted salted cashews

Dressing:
2 tablespoons hoisin sauce
1/3 cup rice vinegar
6 tablespoons vegetable oil
1 teaspoon chili paste with garlic
1/4 cup sugar
2 teaspoons soy sauce

Cut won tons skins into 1/4 inch thick strips. Heat oil in wok or skillet and fry won tons in batches. Drain on paper towels. Whisk together all the dressing ingredients and chill until serving time.

Cut lettuce across into 1/2-inch thick shreds. Cut green onions on a diagonal. Cut red pepper and cucumber into medium dice. Remove skin and bones from chicken and shred. Toss all together in a large bowl and add the won ton crisps, cashews and dressing.

CUBAN CHICKEN SALAD WITH AVOCADOS AND MANGOES

Serves 6.

2 large firm ripe mangoes
2 large avocados
4 cups cooked diced chicken
10 ounces mixed baby greens
3/4 cup toasted cashews

Dressing:
2 cloves garlic
3/4 cup fresh orange juice
2 tablespoons fresh lime juice
1 tablespoon grated orange zest
1 tablespoon honey
1 tablespoon soy sauce

Peel mangoes and cut into medium dice. Peel avocados and cut into medium dice. Rinse avocados in a colander to retard discoloration.

For dressing, peel garlic and mince. Whisk garlic with orange and lime juices, zest, honey and soy sauce. In a medium bowl combine the chicken, mango and avocado. Toss with 1/2 cup dressing. Toss greens with remaining dressing and divide among six plates. Top with chicken mixture and a sprinkling of cashews.

ANTIPASTO CHICKEN SALAD

Serves 4.

**1/4 pound sliced Genoa salami
2 cloves garlic
3 tablespoons fresh lemon juice
1/4 cup olive oil
4 boneless skinless chicken breast halves
3 roasted red peppers
1 (6-ounce) bag baby spinach
6 small radishes, sliced
1/2 cup pitted Kalamata olives
1 medium shallot
4 sprigs fresh Italian parsley
1 tablespoon capers, rinsed and drained
3 tablespoons red wine vinegar
6 tablespoons olive oil**

Preheat oven to 425 degrees. Cut salami in strips and arrange on a parchment lined baking sheet. Bake for 10 minutes or until brown. Cool.

Peel and mince garlic and mix with lemon juice and olive oil. Trim chicken and pound to an even 1/2-inch thickness. Add to garlic mixture and let stand 30 minutes. Grill chicken 4 minutes per side. Cool; cut into strips. Cut roasted peppers into julienne strips.

Chop olives and shallot. Remove parsley leaves and chop. Combine olives and shallot with capers, vinegar, oil and parsley. Toss with spinach, radishes, roasted peppers and salami chips. Serve topped with chicken.

GRILLED CHICKEN, BLACK BEAN AND CORN SALAD WITH SALSA

Serves 4 to 6.

Dressing:
1/4 cup fresh lemon juice
1 tablespoon Dijon mustard
1/2 cup olive oil
2 tablespoons prepared medium salsa

Salad:
4 boneless skinless chicken breast halves
1 large head romaine lettuce
2 medium carrots
1/2 hot house cucumber
2 (15-ounce) cans black beans,
rinsed and drained
1 cup frozen corn, thawed
1 avocado
1 cup crushed blue corn tortilla chips

Whisk together dressing ingredients in a small bowl. Trim chicken and pound to an even 1/2-inch thickness. Pour 1/3 of the dressing over the chicken and let stand 30 minutes. Grill chicken 4 minutes per side. Cut on a diagonal into 1/2-inch thick slices.

Cut lettuce across into 1-inch strips. Peel carrots and thinly slice. Thinly slice the cucumber. Arrange lettuce in a bowl and top with carrots, cucumber, beans, corn and medium diced avocado. Top with chicken and then dressing. Toss and serve topped with chips.

HOISIN PORK AND NAPA SLAW

Serves 4.

**1 head garlic
2 inch piece fresh ginger
6 green onions, divided use
1 pork tenderloin
1/2 cup hoisin sauce
2 tablespoons chili paste with garlic
1/2 cup red wine
1 teaspoon freshly ground pepper**

**Slaw: 1 small bunch basil
1 small head Napa cabbage
2 carrots
1 cup bean sprouts
1/2 cup fish sauce
1/2 cup rice wine vinegar
1-1/2 teaspoons sugar**

Peel and mince garlic and ginger. Chop green onions. Trim pork of all fat and silverskin. Slice pork lengthwise into 3 long thin strips. Mix the garlic, ginger, 1/2 the green onions, hoisin, chili paste, red wine and pepper. Remove and reserve 2 tablespoons. Pour remaining marinade over the pork and let stand 45 minutes. Grill pork 4 to 5 minutes per side. Cut across into thin strips. Stack basil leaves and cut into julienne strips. Cut cabbage into thin strips. Peel carrots and cut into julienne strips. Combine reserved 2 tablespoons marinade with fish sauce, vinegar and sugar. Toss with slaw and pork.

BLACKENED STEAK SALAD WITH PEPPERS, BLUE CHEESE AND DIJON VINAIGRETTE

Serves 6.

2 yellow bell peppers
3 tomatoes
1-1/2 pounds beef top sirloin, 1-inch thick
1/4 cup purchased Steak Rub
2 (6-ounce) bags mixed baby greens
3/4 cup crumbled blue cheese

Dijon Vinaigrette:
2 tablespoons minced green onion
1/2 cup olive oil
1/4 cup balsamic vinegar
2 teaspoons Dijon mustard

Cut yellow peppers into julienne strips. Cut tomatoes lengthwise into wedges. Coat steak on both sides with Steak Rub. Let stand 30 minutes. Grill steak 5 to 6 minutes per side. Remove and set aside to cool slightly. Slice into thin strips across the grain.

Finely mince the green onions. Whisk together Vinaigrette ingredients and toss with lettuce and yellow peppers. Mound salad on serving plates and top with steak slices, blue cheese and tomatoes.

The Art of the KNIFE

The Art of the KNIFE

VEGETARIAN MAIN COURSES

The Art of the KNIFE

COUSCOUS AND FETA CAKES

Serves 6.

**1 small red onion
1 red bell pepper
1/2 yellow bell pepper
2 cloves garlic
3 sprigs fresh dill
3 sprigs Italian parsley
2-1/2 cups water
1 cup couscous
4 tablespoons olive oil
6 ounces crumbled feta cheese
1/2 cup flour
2 eggs, lightly beaten**

Finely dice the onion, red and yellow peppers. Peel and mince the garlic. Remove leaves from dill and parsley sprigs and mince. Heat 1 tablespoon oil in a medium skillet and cook the onion, peppers and garlic until tender. Cool. Bring water to a boil in a medium saucepan and stir in couscous and a pinch salt. Remove from heat and let stand, covered, 10 minutes. Fluff couscous and toss in onion mixture, feta, flour, eggs, dill, parsley, salt and pepper to taste.

Heat 1 tablespoon oil in a nonstick skillet over medium high heat. Drop couscous mixture in 1/3 cup mounds and press slightly to form 3 inch cakes. Cook 3 minutes and turn and cook another 3 minutes or until golden and cooked through. Repeat with remaining oil and couscous.

GREEK GREEN BEAN, ZUCCHINI AND POTATO STEW

Serves 6 to 8.

**1 medium onion
1 pound fresh green beans
1/2 pound medium zucchini
1/2 pound russet potatoes
1 small bunch Italian parsley
1/4 cup olive oil
1/4 teaspoon cayenne pepper
1 (28-ounce) can diced Italian-style tomatoes
1/2 cup crumbled feta cheese**

Chop onion. Trim ends from green beans and cut in half crosswise. Trim ends from zucchini and cut into 1-inch thick slices. Peel potatoes and cut into 1-inch cubes. Remove leaves from parsley and chop.

Heat oil in a large nonstick skillet over medium high heat. Add onion and cook 5 minutes. Add green beans and cayenne and sauté until onions are tender, about 3 minutes. Add zucchini, potatoes and parsley.

Pour on tomatoes and their juices and bring to a boil. Reduce heat, cover and simmer until potatoes are tender stirring frequently, about 45 minutes. Season to taste with salt and pepper. Serve in bowls topped with feta cheese.

The Art of the KNIFE

THAI YAM AND PEPPER CURRY

Serves 4.

**2 red bell peppers
1 medium onion
4 cloves garlic
2 medium orange fleshed yams
1/2 pound snow peas
4 sprigs fresh cilantro
1 tablespoon vegetable oil
1 to 1-1/2 tablespoons Thai green curry paste
1 (14-ounce) can unsweetened coconut milk
1/2 cup water
Cooked jasmine rice**

Cut red peppers into Batonnet strips. Slice the onion lengthwise into thin strips. Peel garlic and mince. Peel yams and cut in half lengthwise. Then cut across into 1/4 inch thick half moons. Trim snow peas and mince cilantro leaves.

Heat oil in a 4 quart pot over medium high heat. Add the bell peppers and onion and cook until tender and beginning to brown, about 5 minutes. Stir in the garlic and curry paste and cook, stirring 1 minute.

Add yams, coconut milk and water and simmer, covered, stirring occasionally, until potatoes are almost tender, about 5 minutes. Add snow peas and simmer, uncovered, until sauce is slightly thickened. Stir in cilantro and serve over rice.

SPANAKOPITA – SPINACH PIE

Serves 8 to 10.

**4 (6-ounce) bags baby spinach leaves
2 bunches green onions
1/2 bunch Italian parsley
1 small bunch fresh dill
1 pound feta cheese, crumbled
8 eggs, lightly beaten
1/2 pound phyllo pastry
3/4 cup olive oil
1 cup unsalted butter, melted**

Coarsely chop the spinach. Trim ends from green onions and chop. Remove parsley and dill leaves and chop.

Heat 1/4 cup olive oil in a medium skillet and cook the green onions until tender, 2 minutes. In a large bowl combine the spinach, green onions, parsley, dill, eggs and feta cheese. Season with salt and pepper and toss together well.

Combine the remaining olive oil and melted butter and use to grease a 9 x 13 inch casserole. Line the casserole with five sheets of phyllo, brushing each sheet with butter mixture. Spread the spinach mixture over phyllo and top with remaining sheets of phyllo with have been brushed with the butter mixture and stacked. Score the top in squares with the tip of a knife down through only 2 or 3 sheets. Bake at 350 degrees for 45 minutes or until well browned. Cool slightly before cutting.

MUSHROOM ENCHILADAS SUIZA

Makes 8.

**1 onion
1 red bell pepper
1 ear fresh corn
3/4 pound mixed mushrooms
1 (4-ounce) can diced green chilies
1/2 cup vegetable oil
8 corn tortillas
2 cups grated Jack cheese
1 cup heavy whipping cream
Cilantro leaves for garnish**

Slice onion lengthwise in thin strips. Cut red pepper into Batonnet strips. Set corn on a dish towel and cut off kernels. Wipe mushrooms clean with a damp paper towel and thinly slice.

Heat oil in a nonstick skillet over medium high heat. Add the tortillas one at a time, turning over almost immediately. Drain tortillas on paper towels.

Add the onion and red pepper to the oil in the skillet and cook 5 minutes. Add the mushrooms and continue cooking 5 to 8 minutes or until all are very tender. Add the chilies and corn and cook 2 minutes. Remove from heat and cool slightly. Season with salt and pepper. Fill tortillas with vegetable filling and all but 1/2 cup cheese. Roll up and arrange in a casserole dish. Pour on cream and top with cheese. Bake 25 minutes at 350 degrees. Top with cilantro to serve.

CHINESE COLD NOODLES

Serves 2 to 3.

8 ounces baked tofu, any flavor
1/2 carrot
1 small red bell pepper
2 green onions
1/2 pound spaghetti
1 tablespoon Asian sesame oil
1 tablespoon toasted sesame seeds

Dressing:
2 slices peeled fresh ginger
1/4 bunch cilantro
1 clove garlic
2 tablespoons rice vinegar
1 teaspoon Dijon mustard
2 teaspoons sugar
1/2 teaspoon salt
1/4 cup vegetable oil

Cut tofu into Batonnet strips. Peel and cut carrot into julienne strips. Cut red pepper into julienne strips. Slice green onions diagonally in thin strips.

Cook spaghetti in a large pot of boiling water. Drain and toss with sesame oil and sesame seeds. Immediately toss with tofu, carrots and red peppers, allowing them to warm and soften slightly.

Combine all dressing ingredients in blender or food processor and pureé. Toss with noodles and sprinkle with green onions.

SPICY ORANGE TOFU NOODLES

Serves 2 to 3.

8 ounces baked tofu, any flavor
1 bunch cilantro
4 slices peeled fresh ginger
4 cloves garlic
1/2 pound linguine
2 teaspoons Asian sesame oil
1 tablespoon vegetable oil

Sauce:
1/4 cup fresh orange juice
1/2 teaspoon grated orange zest
3 tablespoons soy sauce
2 tablespoons spice vinegar
2 tablespoons brown sugar
1 tablespoon Asian sesame oil
1 teaspoon Asian chili sauce
2 teaspoons cornstarch

Cut the tofu into Batonnet strips. Remove cilantro leaves and set aside. Mince ginger and garlic. Combine all sauce ingredients.

Cook linguine in a large pot of boiling water. Drain and toss with sesame oil. Heat vegetable oil in a wok over medium high heat. Add the ginger and garlic and toss 1 minute. Add all the sauce ingredients and tofu and bring to a simmer, stirring often. Cook until sauce is thickened. Toss hot sauce with noodles and cilantro and serve immediately.

BLACK & PINTO BEAN BURGERS

Serves 8.

1/2 medium onion
1/2 carrot, peeled
2 cloves garlic
1 jalapeño chili
3 tablespoons olive oil
1 (15-ounce) can black beans,
rinsed and drained
1 (15-ounce) can pinto beans,
rinsed and drained
1 cup prepared salsa, medium or mild
2 tablespoons self-rising flour or Bisquick
1/2 teaspoon salt
1/2 teaspoon dried oregano
1/2 teaspoon ground cumin
1/2 cup mayonnaise
2 to 3 teaspoons adobo sauce from
canned chipotle chilies
8 whole grain buns, toasted

Finely chop onion and carrot. Peel garlic and mince. Cut chili in half and scoop out seeds and membrane and finely mince. Heat 1 tablespoon oil in a nonstick skillet over medium high heat. Add onion, carrot, garlic and chili and sauté until tender, 5 minutes.

Mash beans and stir in onion mixture, 1/2 cup salsa, flour and spices. Chill 30 minutes. Stir together mayonnaise and adobo sauce and spread on bottom bun. Shape bean mixture into 8 patties. Place on a parchment lined baking pan and brush with oil. Bake at 400 degrees for 15 minutes. Serve on buns and top with remaining salsa.

The Art of the KNIFE

ORANGE PECAN GREEN BEANS

Serves 6.

**1-1/2 pounds fresh green beans
1 large red onion
3/4 cup pecans
1 sprig fresh thyme
6 tablespoons fresh orange juice
2 tablespoons Dijon mustard
1 tablespoon brown sugar
1/4 cup butter**

Trim ends off green beans and cut in half crosswise. Thinly slice the red onion and coarsely chop the pecans. Remove the thyme leaves from stems and mince.

Cook green beans in a large pot of boiling salted water for 5 to 6 minutes. Drain and rinse under cold water to stop cooking. Drain well. In a small bowl, whisk together the orange juice, mustard and brown sugar.

In a large nonstick skillet, melt butter over medium high heat. Add red onion and pecans and toss to coat. Cook, stirring often, until the onions are well browned and pecans are golden, 8 to 10 minutes.

Add green beans and orange juice mixture and thyme. Toss over medium heat until sauce begins to thicken and coats beans well, 3 to 5 minutes. Season to taste with salt and pepper.

GREEN BEANS WITH BACON AND PINE NUTS

Serves 6.

**2 pounds slender green beans
4 slices bacon
1 tablespoon olive oil
1/4 cup toasted pine nuts**

Trim ends off green beans. Cut bacon slices across into 1/2-inch pieces.

Cook green beans in a large pot of boiling salted water for 5 to 6 minutes. Drain and rinse under cold water to stop cooking. Drain well.

Cook bacon in a large skillet over medium heat until crisp, stirring frequently. Using a slotted spoon, remove bacon to paper towels to drain.

Add the olive oil to the bacon drippings and toss in the green beans. Cook, stirring frequently, until beans are lightly browned and tender. Season with salt and pepper. Serve green beans sprinkled with bacon and toasted pine nuts.

JULIENNE CARROTS WITH RASPBERRY GLAZE

Serves 4.

1-1/4 pounds carrots
1 sprig fresh thyme
2 sprigs fresh parsley
3 tablespoons unsalted butter
2 tablespoons raspberry vinegar
1-1/2 tablespoons sugar

Peel carrots and cut into julienne strips. Remove thyme and parsley leaves from stems and chop.

In a medium to large skillet melt the butter over medium heat. Stir in the raspberry vinegar, sugar and thyme. Let the mixture simmer for 1 minute until slightly thickened.

Stir in the carrots and toss to coat well with the glaze. Cover the pan and cook the carrots for 1 to 2 minutes. Uncover and continue cooking, tossing often, until tender and well glazed, about 3 minutes. Season with salt and pepper. Serve sprinkled with parsley.

JULIENNE ZUCCHINI WITH TOMATOES

Serves 6.

6 medium zucchini (about 2-1/2 pounds)
2 teaspoons salt
1 clove garlic, minced
1/2 medium onion
2 plum tomatoes
2 tablespoons unsalted butter
1 tablespoon olive oil
Freshly ground pepper

Cut zucchini into julienne or batonnet strips. Toss zucchini with salt in a colander and let drain for 20 to 30 minutes. Lightly rinse, drain and squeeze dry without crushing zucchini.

Peel and mince garlic. Chop onion. Cut tomatoes lengthwise into quarters. Scoop out seeds and cut tomatoes into medium dice.

Melt butter with olive oil in a large skillet over medium high heat. Sauté the garlic and onion until tender, 3 minutes. Add the zucchini and cook until zucchini is crisp-tender and turns a brighter green color, 5 to 7 minutes. Season with pepper. Toss in the tomatoes and cook until warmed through, about 3 minutes. Serve immediately.

The Art of the KNIFE

LEMONY RICE PILAF WITH PARMESAN CHEESE

Serves 6 to 8.

1 large onion
4 sprigs fresh parsley
1/4 cup unsalted butter
2 cups long grain white rice
Pinch saffron threads
4 cups chicken broth
1/2 teaspoon salt
1/2 teaspoon freshly ground pepper
Grated zest of 2 lemons
1/3 cup freshly grated Parmesan cheese

Chop onion. Remove parsley leaves from stems and chop.

Melt butter in a heavy 3 quart saucepan. Sauté the onions until transparent. Add the rice and toss in the butter-onion mixture over medium heat for 2 minutes.

Add the broth and saffron, salt and pepper and bring to a boil. Stir, cover and lower heat. Cook 18 to 22 minutes or until rice has absorbed all the liquid. Fluff the rice and toss in the lemon zest and cheese. Serve sprinkled with parsley.

TOASTED GARLIC RICE WITH FRESH HERBS

Serves 6.

1/2 bunch fresh cilantro
1/2 bunch Italian parsley
4 sprigs fresh oregano
12 cloves garlic
2 tablespoons vegetable oil
1-1/2 cups long grain white rice
3 cups chicken broth
2 tablespoons fresh lime juice
1/2 teaspoon salt
1-1/2 teaspoons grated lime zest

Remove cilantro, parsley and oregano leaves from stems and mince. Set aside. Peel and mince garlic.

Heat oil in a large saucepan over medium heat. Add garlic and sauté until golden, being careful not to burn. Add rice and stir 2 minutes or until glossy. Add broth and lime juice and salt and bring to a boil. Stir; reduce heat and cook, covered, until rice is tender, 18 to 22 minutes.

Turn off heat and let stand 5 minutes. Add herbs and lime zest and fluff with a fork.

GARLIC MASHED POTATOES

Serves 4 to 6.

2-1/2 pounds russet potatoes
6 cloves garlic, peeled
2 teaspoons salt
1/4 cup butter, cut up
1 cup sour cream or more
Salt and pepper to taste

Peel potatoes and quarter. Place in a large pot of cold water. Peel garlic cloves and add to pot. Bring the water to a boil and then add the 2 teaspoons salt. Continue cooking 15 minutes or until potatoes are very tender.

Place the butter and sour cream in the bottom of a large bowl. Force the potatoes and cooked garlic cloves through a ricer into the bowl. Stir to incorporate, adding more sour cream as needed. Season to taste with salt and pepper.

CREAMY BASIL POTATO MASH

Makes 2 cups.

Pesto: 2 cloves garlic
1 cup fresh basil leaves
1 cup fresh spinach leaves
3 green onions
3 tablespoons pine nuts
1/4 cup freshly grated Parmesan
1/2 teaspoon salt
1/3 to 1/2 cup extra-virgin olive oil

3 pounds russet potatoes
4 tablespoons unsalted butter
3/4 to 1 cup heavy cream, heated
Salt and pepper to taste

Peel garlic. Coarsely chop basil, spinach and green onions. To make the pesto, drop the garlic cloves into a running food processor and process until minced. Stop machine and add spinach, basil, green onion, pine nuts, Parmesan and salt. Pulse to chop. With machine running, add the olive oil to make a paste.

Peel potatoes and quarter. Place potatoes in a large pot and cover with cold water. Bring to a boil and add 1 teaspoon salt. Continue to simmer until potatoes are tender, about 15 minutes. Force potatoes through a ricer into a large bowl and stir in the butter and enough cream to make moist rice mashed potatoes. Season with salt and pepper. Swirl pesto through mashed potatoes and serve immediately.

CHUNKY POTATOES WITH TWO CHEESES AND GARLIC

Serves 6- 8.

**4 pounds russet potatoes
2 heads garlic
2 small shallots
1/4 cup oil-packed sun-dried tomatoes, drained
2 cups heavy whipping cream
2 tablespoons prepared pesto sauce
1/4 teaspoon white pepper
1-1/2 cups grated mozzarella cheese
1-1/2 cups grated Emmentaler (Swiss) cheese**

Peel potatoes and cut into 1/2-inch cubes. Place potatoes in a greased 13 x 9 inch baking dish. Cover with plastic wrap and cook in the microwave oven on HIGH power for 16 minutes, stirring every 4 minutes or until potatoes are just about tender.

Peel garlic and mince. Chop shallots. Mix cream, sun-dried tomatoes, shallots, garlic, pesto and white pepper in a large bowl. Pour over potatoes; stir gently to coat. Sprinkle both cheeses over potato mixture.

Bake at 375 degrees until potatoes are very tender and cheese is golden brown on top, about 45 minutes. Let cool about 10 minutes before serving.

ARTICHOKE AND POTATO FRITTATA

Serves 4- 6.

**1-1/2 pounds small white rose or red potatoes
1 medium onion
1 roasted red pepper
1 (15-ounce) can artichokes, rinsed and drained
2 tablespoons chopped fresh basil
2 tablespoons chopped fresh parsley
2 tablespoons olive oil
12 large eggs
1/3 cup freshly grated Parmesan
Salt and pepper to taste**

Place potatoes in a large pot and cover with cold water. Bring to a boil and cook for about 15 minutes or until tender. Cool, then cut into 1/2-inch thick slices.

Chop onion and cut roasted pepper into julienne strips. Slice artichoke hearts in strips. Stack basil leaves and chop. Remove parsley leaves from stems and chop. Sauté onion in olive oil to soften. Spread in an oiled 9 x 13 inch dish. Add the potatoes to the skillet; cook for 3 to 5 minutes, turning them often, until browned. Arrange potatoes over the onions. Scatter the roasted pepper, artichoke hearts, basil and parsley on top.

In a medium bowl, whisk the eggs, Parmesan, salt and pepper. Pour over the vegetables. Bake for 30 to 35 minutes or until eggs are set. Serve hot or warm.

The Art of the KNIFE

The Art of the KNIFE

POULTRY
MEATS
and SEAFOOD

GRILLED CHICKEN BREASTS WITH SMOKY CORN SALSA

Serves 8.

**1 bunch cilantro
1 small red onion
1 red bell pepper
2 serrano chilies
3 ears fresh corn
4 teaspoons minced chipotle chilies
in adobo sauce
1/2 cup fresh lime juice
2/3 cup corn oil
8 boneless skinless chicken breast halves**

Remove cilantro leaves and finely chop. Dice the red onion and bell pepper. Remove stem from chilies and mince, seeds and all.

Remove husks and silk from corn and grill ears quickly, turning them so they cook and color evenly, for about 5 minutes. Cool. Cut corn from cobs and toss with diced onion, peppers and chilies. Season to taste with salt and pepper. Let stand for 30 minutes before serving.

Meanwhile, trim chicken and pound between two sheets of plastic wrap to an even 1/2-inch thickness. Whisk together chipotle chilies, lime juice, corn oil and cilantro. Pour over chicken, turing to coat and refrigerate, covered, for 2 hours. Grill chicken 4 minutes per side. Serve topped with corn salsa.

PEPPER JELLY GLAZED CHICKEN

Serves 4.

**6 plum tomatoes
1 pound medium zucchini
1 bunch cilantro
1 medium onion
4 cloves garlic
3 ears corn
1 tablespoon unsalted butter
2 tablespoons jalapeño pepper jelly
4 teaspoons fresh lime juice
1/2 teaspoon chili powder
4 boneless skinless chicken breast halves
3 tablespoons cream cheese**

Cut tomatoes into quarters lengthwise and cut out seeds. Cut into medium dice. Cut the zucchini to medium dice. Finely chop cilantro. Finely chop onion. Peel and mince garlic. Cut corn from cobs.

Melt butter in a large skillet and sauté the onion for 3 minutes. Add the tomatoes, zucchini, garlic and corn and cook, covered, until zucchini is tender, about 15 minutes. Stir in cream cheese.

Trim chicken and pound between two sheets of plastic wrap to an even 1/2-inch thickness. Melt pepper jelly and stir in lime juice and chili powder. Divide in half, setting one aside. Brush chicken with half the jelly and grill 4 minutes per side. Brush with remaining glaze. Serve chicken topped with corn.

LEMONGRASS CHICKEN BREASTS

Serves 6.

**4 stalks lemongrass
10 cloves garlic
5 shallots
4 serrano chilies
6 chicken breast halves with skin and bones
1/2 cup water
2 tablespoons sugar
1 tablespoon fish sauce
2 tablespoons olive oil**

Trim stem ends from lemongrass and slice across to the green tops. Peel garlic. Peel and quarter shallots. Trim stem ends from chilies and cut in half.

Wash and thoroughly dry chicken breasts. Combine all remaining ingredients in blender and pureé. Place chicken in a bowl and pour on marinade. Cover and refrigerate 24 hours.

Preheat oven to 375 degrees. Remove chicken from marinade and arrange on a parchment lined baking sheet. Bake chicken for 50 to 60 minutes or until chicken is cooked through.

CHIPOTLE CHICKEN THIGHS

Serves 4 to 8.

1 clove garlic
4 sprigs cilantro
8 chicken thighs
1 cup plain yogurt
2 tablespoons minced chipotle peppers in adobo
2 tablespoons fresh lime juice
1/2 teaspoon salt

Peel garlic and mince. Remove cilantro leaves from stems and mince. Stir garlic and cilantro into yogurt. Stir in chipotle chilies, lime juice and salt.

Remove skin from chicken thighs, wash and thoroughly dry chicken. Place in a casserole dish. Pour yogurt mixture over the chicken, turning to coat each piece. Cover and refrigerate for at least 8 hours and up to 24 hours.

Preheat oven to 375 degrees. Remove thighs from the marinade and arrange on a parchment lined baking sheet. Bake for 50 to 60 minutes or until cooked through.

The Art of the KNIFE

GREEK CHICKEN BUNDLES

Serves 6.

1 clove garlic
3 sprigs fresh oregano
1 large tomato
1/4 red bell pepper
1/4 cucumber
1 green onion
1/2 cup crumbled feta cheese
4 tablespoons olive oil, divided use
2 teaspoons wine vinegar
6 boneless skinless chicken breast halves
2 eggs, lightly beaten
1-1/2 cups croutons, crushed

Peel and mince garlic. Remove leaves from oregano and mince. Cut tomato in half crosswise, squeeze out the seeds and cut into medium dice. Cut red pepper and cucumber into medium dice. Chop the green onion. Combine all with feta, 1 tablespoon olive oil and vinegar in a small bowl.

Wash and thoroughly dry chicken breasts. Trim chicken and pound between two sheets of plastic wrap to an even 1/4-inch thickness. Divide filling among chicken and fold over to enclose, pressing edges to seal. Dip in egg and then in croutons.

Preheat oven to 425 degrees. Heat 3 tablespoons olive oil on a baking sheet in oven for 4 minutes. Add chicken and cook 8 minutes; turn and cook 8 to 10 minutes longer or until cooked through.

GOAT CHEESE AND PEPPER STUFFED CHICKEN BREASTS

Serves 6.

**1 roasted red pepper
1 shallot
2 cloves garlic
1 sprig fresh rosemary
4 ounces goat cheese
6 boneless skinless chicken breast halves
2 eggs, lightly beaten
1-1/2 cups plain dry bread crumbs
4 tablespoons olive oil**

Cut roasted pepper in strips and set aside. Mince shallot and peel and mince garlic. Remove leaves from rosemary and mince.

Wash and thoroughly dry chicken breasts. Trim chicken and pound between two sheets of plastic wrap to an even 1/4-inch thickness. Divide pepper, shallot, garlic, rosemary and goat cheese among chicken and fold over to enclose, pressing edges to seal. Dip in egg and then in breadcrumbs.

Preheat oven to 425 degrees. Heat olive on a baking sheet in oven for 4 minutes. Add chicken and cook 8 minutes; turn and cook 8 to 10 minutes longer or until cooked through.

CAJUN CHICKEN BREASTS WITH CREAMY CREOLE SAUCE

Serves 6.

1/2 small onion
1 rib celery
1/4 green bell pepper
4 plum tomatoes
6 sprigs fresh oregano
6 sprigs fresh thyme
3 tablespoons unsalted butter
1 teaspoon plus 2 tablespoons
Cajun/Creole spice
1 teaspoon sugar
1/4 cup dry white wine
2 teaspoons Louisiana hot sauce
1/2 cup heavy whipping cream
6 boneless skinless chicken breast halves
2 tablespoons vegetable oil

Finely dice onion to make 1/4 cup. Finely dice celery and green pepper to make 1/4 cup each. Cut tomatoes in quarters lengthwise, scoop out the seeds and cut into medium dice. Remove leaves from oregano and thyme and mince.

Melt butter in a medium skillet over medium heat. Add onion, celery and green pepper and cook until tender, about 5 minutes. Stir in 1 teaspoon Cajun/Creole spice and sugar and toss well. Add wine and bring to a boil.

Stir in tomatoes and hot sauce, simmering until tomatoes soften, about 5 minutes. Add fresh herbs and cream. Salt and pepper to taste. Keep warm.

Preheat grill. Trim chicken and pound to an even 1/2-inch thickness between two sheets of plastic wrap. Season well using 2 tablespoons Cajun/Creole spice. Let stand at room temperature 20 to 30 minutes. Brush with oil and grill 4 minutes per side.

Reheat sauce, if necessary, and spoon over chicken to serve.

SHIITAKE MUSHROOM STUFFED POCKET CHICKEN

Serves 6.

2 green onions
1/2 pound shiitake mushrooms
6 boneless skinless chicken breast halves
4 tablespoons unsalted butter
1 cup purchased Teriyaki Sauce

Trim ends from green onions and finely chop. Remove stems from shiitake mushrooms and thinly slice. Melt 2 tablespoons butter in a medium skillet over medium high heat. Add the green onion and toss to wilt, 1 minute. Add the mushrooms and cook for 3 to 5 minutes or until wilted and tender. Season to taste with salt and pepper. Cool completely.

Wash and thoroughly dry the chicken breasts. Cut a pocket in the side of each breast about 2 inches long. Spoon the mushrooms into the chicken pockets and secure edges with toothpicks.

Melt remaining 2 tablespoons butter in a large skillet over medium high heat. Add the chicken and brown well, about 3 minutes per side. Reduce heat to medium low and add the Teriyaki sauce to the pan. Cover and cook chicken until cooked through, about 8 to 10 minutes, turning chicken once to glaze both sides.

BLUE CHEESE AND BACON STUFFED POCKET CHICKEN

Serves 6.

**1 green onion
3 slices bacon
3/4 cup crumbled blue cheese
6 boneless skinless chicken breast halves
2 eggs, lightly beaten
1-1/2 cups plain dry breadcrumbs
1 teaspoon paprika
4 tablespoons vegetable oil**

Trim ends from green onion and finely chop. Cut bacon across into thin strips. Cook bacon in a nonstick skillet over medium high heat until crispy. Transfer to paper towels to drain.

Wash and thoroughly dry the chicken breasts. Cut a pocket in the side of each breast about 2 inches long.

Mix bacon, green onion and blue cheese together and stuff into the chicken pockets. Secure each with a toothpick. Coat chicken in the eggs and then dredge in the breadcrumbs mixed with paprika to make a thick crust.

Preheat oven to 425 degrees. Heat oil on a baking sheet 4 minutes. Add chicken and cook 7 minutes, turn and cook 7 to 9 minutes longer or until chicken is cooked through.

ITALIAN CHICKEN BREASTS

Serves 6.

**4 cloves garlic
2 shallots
6 sprigs fresh thyme
1/2 pound mushrooms
1 bunch green onions
3 plum tomatoes
6 skinless boneless chicken breast halves
3/4 cup flour
2 tablespoons olive oil
1/2 cup dry white wine
1 cup chicken broth**

Peel garlic and mince. Chop shallots and mix with garlic. Remove leaves from thyme and mince. Wipe mushrooms clean with a damp paper towel, trim ends and slice. Trim ends from green onions and slice across. Quarter tomatoes lengthwise, scoop out seeds and cut into medium dice.

Trim chicken and pound between two sheets of plastic wrap to an even 1/2-inch thickness. Season chicken with salt and pepper and dredge in flour to coat, shaking off excess. Heat oil in a large skillet over medium high heat. Brown chicken 2 minutes per side. Remove to a plate. Add garlic, shallots, thyme and mushrooms and cook for 5 minutes. Add wine and bring to a boil, scraping up any brown bits. Add chicken broth, green onions and tomatoes. Add chicken and simmer 8 minutes or until cooked through. Serve chicken with sauce.

CHICKEN SALTIMBOCCA

Serves 6.

**2 cloves garlic
6 fresh sage leaves
1/2 pound mushrooms
6 skinless boneless chicken breast halves
3/4 cup flour
2 tablespoons olive oil
2 tablespoons unsalted butter
1/2 cup dry white wine
1/2 cup chicken broth
6 thin slices prosciutto
6 thin slices provolone cheese**

Peel garlic and mince. Stack sage leaves and thinly slice across. Wipe mushrooms clean with a damp paper towel, trim ends and slice.

Trim chicken and pound between two sheets of plastic wrap to an even 1/2-inch thickness. Season chicken with salt and pepper and dredge in flour to coat, shaking off excess. Heat oil with butter in a large skillet over medium high heat. Brown chicken 2 minutes per side. Remove to a plate. Add garlic, sage and mushrooms and cook for 5 minutes. Add wine and chicken broth and bring to a boil, scraping up any brown bits. Add chicken, cover and simmer 8 minutes or until cooked through. Top each chicken breast with a slice of prosciutto and cheese. Cover and heat 1 minute longer to melt cheese. Serve chicken with sauce.

The Art of the KNIFE

ALMOND CURRY CHICKEN BREASTS WITH YOGURT SAUCE

Serves 4.

**1/2 cup chopped almonds
3 sprigs fresh cilantro
4 skinless boneless chicken breast halves
1/2 cup flour
1 egg mixed with 1/4 cup milk
1 cup soft fresh breadcrumbs
1-1/2 teaspoons curry powder
1/4 cup vegetable oil**

**Yogurt Sauce:
8 ounces plain yogurt
3 sprigs fresh cilantro
1 tablespoon honey**

Coarsely chop almonds. Remove cilantro leaves from stems and mince. Trim chicken and pound to an even 1/2-inch thickness. Combine the breadcrumbs, almonds, cilantro and curry powder on a plate. To make yogurt sauce, stir together yogurt, minced cilantro and honey.

Preheat oven to 400 degrees. Heat the oil in a large nonstick skillet over medium high heat. Coat chicken with flour, shaking off excess. Dip in egg mixture, coating well and then dredge in nut mixture forming a thick coating. Cook chicken in hot oil to brown only, about 2 minutes per side. Transfer to a baking sheet and cook for 6 to 8 minutes in the oven to finish cooking through. Serve topped with Yogurt Sauce.

CRANBERRY CHICKEN BREASTS

Serves 8.

**1 small onion
8 boneless skinless chicken breast halves
3 tablespoons unsalted butter
1/3 cup brown sugar
1-1/2 tablespoons cider vinegar
1 teaspoon powdered mustard
2/3 cup ketchup
2 cups fresh or frozen cranberries**

Chop onion. Trim chicken and pound between two sheets of plastic wrap to an even thickness of 1/4 inch. Melt 2 tablespoons butter in a large skillet over medium high heat. Add the chicken and brown 2 minutes on each side. Remove the chicken to a plate and set aside.

Add the remaining butter to the skillet and cook the onion until tender. Add the ketchup, brown sugar, vinegar, mustard and cranberries. Cook, stirring often, until cranberries pop and sauce thickens, about 8 minutes.

Return chicken to the skillet and coat well in the sauce. Cover and simmer over low heat for 8 to 10 minutes or until the chicken is cooked through.

CHICKEN AND ASPARAGUS TOSS

Serves 4 to 6.

**2 shallots
1 pound asparagus
3 sprigs fresh tarragon
1-1/2 pound boneless skinless chicken breasts
1/4 cup flour
2 tablespoons vegetable oil, divided use
1/3 cup dry white wine
1 cup chicken broth
1/3 cup sour cream
2 tablespoons Dijon mustard**

Finely chop shallots. Trim asparagus ends and cut on a diagonal into 1-inch lengths. Remove leaves from tarragon and mince. Trim chicken and cut into Batonnet strips. Season chicken with salt and pepper and toss in flour.

Heat 1 tablespoon oil in a wok or large skillet over medium high heat. Toss chicken until browned, about 5 minutes. Remove to a bowl. Add remaining oil and shallots. Cook briefly and then add the asparagus and 1/2 cup broth. Boil asparagus about 3 minutes. Remove to another bowl.

Return chicken to pan; add remaining broth and wine. Simmer for 2 to 3 minutes. In a small bowl whisk the sour cream, mustard and tarragon. Stir into chicken and heat through, but do not boil. Stir in asparagus and season to taste. Serve immediately.

GINGER CHICKEN TOSS

Serves 6.

**1 onion
5 cloves garlic
1-1/2 inches fresh ginger root
6 sprigs fresh mint
8 large shiitake mushrooms
5 green onions
1/2 red bell pepper
1-1/2 pounds boneless skinless chicken breasts
3 tablespoons vegetable oil
2 tablespoons soy sauce
1/2 teaspoon crushed red pepper flakes
2 tablespoons rice vinegar
1 teaspoon sugar
2 tablespoons fish sauce**

Thinly slice onion lengthwise. Peel and mince garlic. Peel ginger and mince. Stack mint leaves and slice across into thin strips. Remove stems from shiitake mushrooms and slice across into thin slices. Cut green onions in one inch lengths. Cut red pepper in medium julienne. Trim chicken and cut into Batonnet strips.

Heat 1 tablespoon oil in wok and cook onions 3 minutes. Add garlic and toss 1 minute. Remove to a bowl. Add remaining oil and chicken; toss 3 minutes. Toss in soy sauce, ginger and mint. Add mushrooms, green onions, red pepper, red pepper flakes and cooked onions and cook until chicken is tender. Add vinegar, sugar and fish sauce. Serve.

CHICKEN, POTATO AND GREEN BEAN AND BASIL TOSS

Serves 4.

**3/4 pound small white potatoes
6 ounces thin green beans
4 boneless skinless chicken breast halves
1 large shallot
2 cloves garlic
4 sun-dried tomatoes in oil, drained
1 lemon
6 basil leaves
2 tablespoons flour
3 tablespoons olive oil
1/4 cup dry red wine
12 Kalamata olives**

Cut potatoes into thin wedges. Cut green beans into 1-1/2-inch lengths. Trim chicken and cut into one inch wide strips. Finely chop shallot. Peel garlic and mince. Slice sun-dried tomatoes into julienne strips. Slice lemon and stack basil leaves and cut into thin stirps.

Steam potatoes for 5 minutes. Add green beans and steam another 5 minutes or until vegetables are tender. Drain and set aside. Toss chicken with flour. Heat oil in large nonstick skillet or wok. Cook shallot and garlic 1 minute. Add chicken and cook 4 minutes. Add sun-dried tomatoes, lemon slices and olives; cover and cook 2 minutes. Add potatoes and green beans and toss until heated through. Add basil and toss to combine.

CHICKEN WITH ARTICHOKES AND PROSCIUTTO

Serves 4.

1 small onion
1 clove garlic
1 sprig fresh rosemary
3 sprigs fresh thyme
6 fresh basil leaves
1-1/4 pounds boneless skinless chicken breasts
2 ounces prosciutto slices
1 (6-ounce) jar marinated artichoke hearts
1/3 cup Kalamata olives
3 tablespoons olive oil, divided use
Pinch crushed red pepper flakes
1/3 cup chicken broth
3 tablespoons dry white wine
1 cup frozen tiny peas, thawed

Finely chop onion. Peel and mince garlic. Remove leaves from rosemary and thyme stems and mince. Stack basil leaves and chop. Trim chicken and cut into 1-inch cubes. Coarsely chop prosciutto. Drain artichoke hearts and coarsely chop. Pit and quarter olives.

Heat half the oil in large skillet or wok over medium heat. Season chicken and toss in pan 4 minutes. Remove to a bowl. Add remaining oil and the onion, garlic, prosciutto and red pepper flakes. Toss 1-1/2 minutes. Add artichokes, broth, olives, wine, rosemary and thyme. cook 1 minutes. Return chicken to pan add peas and heat until cooked through. Remove from heat and toss in basil.

The Art of the KNIFE

SAFFRON CHICKEN AND SAUSAGES

Serves 6.

**2 large cloves garlic
2 medium zucchini
1 roasted red pepper
3 sprigs Italian parsley
1-1/2 pounds boneless skinless chicken breasts
3/4 pound sweet Italian sausages
1/4 cup flour
3 tablespoons olive oil, divided use
1 tablespoon unsalted butter
1/4 teaspoon crushed red pepper flakes
1/4 cup dry white wine
1/2 cup chicken broth
Pinch saffron threads**

Peel and slice garlic cloves. Cut zucchini and roasted pepper into Batonnet strips. Remove parsley leaves and mince. Trim chicken and cut into 1/2-inch thick strips.

Pierce sausages and place in a pan of cold water. Bring to a boil and then simmer 10 minutes. Remove and cool. Slice sausages into 1/2-inch slices.

Season chicken with salt and pepper and toss with flour. Heat 2 tablespoons olive oil in large skillet over medium high heat. Add zucchini and toss 3 to 5 minutes to brown. Remove with a slotted spoon to a bowl.

Add sausage slices to skillet and cook until nicely brown. Remove to a bowl. Add remaining oil and butter to skillet. Add pepper flakes and garlic and then chicken. Cook chicken, tossing continuously, for 3 to 4 minutes or until browned. Add wine and bring to a boil, scraping up any bits from bottom of pan. Add chicken broth and saffron and simmer 3 to 4 minutes.

Return sausages and zucchini to pan. Add roasted red peppers. Toss and simmer over low heat until warmed through. Sprinkle with parsley to serve.

The Art of the KNIFE

THAI GINGER CHICKEN

Serves 2 to 4.

**4 dried shiitake mushrooms
1 clove garlic
2 inch piece ginger root
2 shallots
1 serrano chili
1 onion
1/2 red bell pepper
2 sprigs fresh cilantro
1/2 pound boneless skinless chicken breasts
3 tablespoons vegetable oil
1 tablespoon oyster sauce
1 tablespoon fish sauce
1/2 teaspoon sugar
Pinch white pepper**

Soak dried mushrooms in hot water for 30 minutes. Drain, remove stems and thinly slice. Peel and mince the garlic and ginger. Chop shallots and slice chili and onion. Cut bell pepper in julienne strips. Remove cilantro leaves and mince.

Heat 1 tablespoon oil in wok and toss in shallots, chili, onions, red pepper and mushrooms. Toss 3 minutes or until tender. Remove to a plate. Add remaining oil and garlic and ginger. Cook 1 minute. Add chicken and toss until cooked through, 4 minutes. Add oyster and fish sauces, sugar and pepper and toss to combine. Toss in cooked vegetables and season to taste. Sprinkle with cilantro to serve.

THAI STYLE
TURKEY BURGERS

Serves 4.

**1 large clove garlic
1 slice peeled fresh ginger root
1/2 bunch fresh cilantro
6 sprigs fresh mint leaves
12 fresh basil leaves
2 tablespoons fresh lime juice
2 teaspoons sugar
1 pound ground turkey
3 tablespoons fresh breadcrumbs
1/2 teaspoon cayenne, or to taste
1 teaspoon paprika**

Peel garlic. Remove leaves from cilantro and mint stems. Into a food processor with the motor on, drop the garlic and the ginger slice. Stop and add the cilantro, mint, basil, lime juice, sugar and blend the mixture well. In a bowl combine the turkey, the herb mixture, the breadcrumbs, and the cayenne and form the mixture into four 1-inch thick patties.

Preheat grill. Sprinkle patties with paprika and grill for 7 to 8 minutes per side or until cooked through.

GINGER CHICKEN SATAY

Makes 16.

**1 large bunch cilantro
1 large head garlic
1-inch piece ginger root
1/4 cup vegetable oil
2 tablespoons water
3 tablespoons fish sauce
2 tablespoons sugar
1/2 teaspoon ground white pepper
4 boneless skinless chicken breast halves
Cucumber Salad (see page 130)**

Cut cilantro off above rubber band, saving both leaves and stems. Peel garlic cloves. Peel ginger and slice. Place cilantro, garlic and ginger in food processor and pulse to mince well. With processor running pour in oil, fish sauce, water, sugar and white pepper.

Trim chicken and cut each into four long strips. Place chicken in a bowl and toss with cilantro mixture. Let stand for 30 minutes and then place chicken on bamboo skewers which have soaked in cold water for 20 minutes. Grill or broil chicken for 4 to 5 minutes per side. Serve with Cucumber Salad.

SOUTHWESTERN CHICKEN KABOBS

Makes 4.

**2 jalapeño chilies
2 cloves garlic
4 sprigs cilantro
2 tablespoons honey
1/2 cup fresh lime juice
1/4 cup olive oil
4 large boneless skinless chicken breast halves
Salsa Fresca (see page 32) or
Strawberry Salsa (see page 33)**

Trim ends from jalapeños and slice. Peel garlic. Remove cilantro leaves. Place jalapeño chilies, garlic and cilantro in food processor and pulse to mince well. Add the honey, lime juice and olive oil and process to pureé.

Trim chicken and cut into 1-inch cubes. Place in a bowl and toss with jalapeño mixture. Let stand for 30 minutes. Thread chicken on bamboo skewers which have been soaked in cold water for 20 minutes. Grill or broil chicken for 4 to 5 minutes per side. Serve with Salsa Fresca or Strawberry Salsa.

PORK CHOPS WITH BACON AND MUSHROOMS

Serves 4 to 6.

1/2 pound white mushrooms
2 medium onions
1/4 pound bacon slices
2 tablespoons unsalted butter
4 to 6 pork chops with bones (3/4 inches thick)
2 tablespoons flour
1-1/2 teaspoons paprika
1 cup beef broth
1 cup whipping cream
2 tablespoons tomato sauce

Wipe mushrooms clean with a damp paper towel and cut into quarters. Coarsely chop onions. Slice bacon across in thin strips.

Preheat oven to 375 degrees. Melt butter in large skillet over medium high heat. Season pork chops with salt and pepper and brown 4 minutes per side. Transfer chops to a baking dish and sprinkle mushrooms on top.

Add onions and bacon to skillet and cook until bacon is crisp, stirring frequently, about 10 minutes. Mix in flour and paprika. Stir in broth and cream and bring to a boil, stirring constantly. Mix in tomato sauce. Season with salt and pepper and pour over chops. Bake for 20 to 25 minutes or until chops are tender and cooked through.

ROSEMARY AND RASPBERRY VINEGAR PORK CHOPS

Serves 4.

**3 cloves garlic
4 sprigs rosemary
2 tablespoons flour
1/4 teaspoon salt
1/4 teaspoon white pepper
4 large center cut pork chops
2 tablespoons olive oil
1/2 cup beef broth
1/2 cup dry vermouth
6 small sprigs of rosemary
1/4 cup raspberry vinegar
1/2 cup whipping cream**

Peel and mince garlic. Remove leaves from one sprig rosemary and mince enough to make 1/2 teaspoon. Toss minced rosemary with flour, salt and white pepper. Coat pork chops with flour mixture.

Heat oil in a large skillet and sauté garlic for 1 minute. Add chops and brown chops 4 minutes per side. Add broth and vermouth and remaining 3 rosemary sprigs. Bring to simmer, cover and cook for 35 to 40 minutes or until chops are tender when pierced with a knife. Remove chops to a plate and keep warm. Remove rosemary.

Add vinegar to sauce and boil to reduce by half. Add cream and boil until slightly thickened. Season with salt and pepper and serve sauce over chops.

ARISTA PORK TENDERLOIN

Serves 8 to 10.

**15 large cloves garlic
6 sprigs fresh rosemary
1 tablespoon salt
1 tablespoon freshly ground pepper
1/2 cup olive oil
4 pork tenderloins**

Peel garlic. Remove leaves from rosemary stems. With food processor running, drop in garlic cloves and process until minced. Stop machine and add the rosemary, salt and pepper. With machine running slowly add the olive oil and process to form a paste.

Trim pork of all fat and silverskin. Rub the garlic paste all over the pork and let stand at room temperature for 30 to 60 minutes.

Preheat oven to 375 degrees. Place pork on parchment lined baking sheets and roast for 25 to 30 minutes or until an internal temperature of 155 degrees is reached. Let stand about 7 minutes. Slice on a diagonal and serve.

PORK TENDERLOIN WITH ASSORTED MUSHROOMS

Serves 4 to 5.

**1 pound assorted mushrooms
(crimini, button, shiitake, etc.)
1/2 bunch chives
3 sprigs tarragon
4 sprigs Italian parsley
2 pork tenderloins
2 tablespoons olive oil
1 cup chicken broth
1/2 cup Madeira wine
2 tablespoons unsalted butter
1/2 cup heavy cream**

Wipe mushrooms clean with a damp paper towel and remove stems. Slice mushrooms. Chop chives, tarragon and parsley and set aside.

Preheat oven to 400 degrees. Trim pork tenderloins of all fat and silverskin. Heat oil in a large skillet over medium high heat. Brown pork all around, about 6 minutes total. Transfer pork to a baking dish. Add broth and Madeira to skillet and boil until reduced by half. Pour over pork and bake 25 to 30 minutes.

Add butter to pork skillet and sauté the mushrooms until softened and browned lightly. Pour juices from pork dish into mushrooms and add the cream. Boil to thicken slightly. Stir in herbs and season to taste. Pour sauce over sliced pork to serve.

PORK TENDERLOIN WITH HONEY GINGER SAUCE

Serves 4 to 5.

**2-inch piece fresh ginger
1 shallot
2 cloves garlic
2 pork tenderloins
2 tablespoons honey
3 tablespoons vegetable oil
1 tablespoon Asian sesame oil
1 cup chicken broth
1/2 cup dry white wine
2 teaspoons fresh lemon juice**

Peel ginger, slice and then finely mince. Peel and thinly slice shallot. Peel and mince garlic.

Trim pork tenderloins of all fat and silverskin. Stir together 2 tablespoons minced ginger and honey. Season pork with salt and pepper and spread honey all over. Let stand 30 minutes. Preheat oven to 400 degrees.

Heat oil in a large skillet over medium high heat. Brown pork on all sides, about 6 minutes total. Transfer to a parchment lined baking sheet and roast 25 minutes. Let stand 5 minutes; then slice.

Meanwhile, heat sesame oil in the pork skillet and sauté shallot, garlic and 1 tablespoon minced ginger for 1 to 2 minutes. Add broth, wine and lemon juice; bring to a boil and reduce by half. Serve sauce over pork.

SPICY SWEET SOUR PORK

Makes 2 to 4.

**Pork and marinade: 1 pound pork tenderloin
1 tablespoon dark soy sauce
1 tablespoon hoisin sauce
1 tablespoon dry sherry
1 tablespoon Asian sesame oil
1/2 teaspoon Asian chili sauce**

**Lemon Sauce: 1 tablespoon lemon zest
1 tablespoon minced fresh ginger
1/3 cup chicken broth
3 tablespoons fresh lemon juice
1 tablespoon thin soy sauce
2 tablespoons honey
2 teaspoons cornstarch
2 teaspoons Asian chili sauce**

**2 tablespoons vegetable oil
3 cloves garlic, minced
1 tablespoon minced fresh ginger
2 whole green onions, slivered**

Trim pork of all fat and silverskin and then cut into julienne strips. Place pork in a bowl and add the marinade ingredients. Set aside for 30 minutes. Stir together sauce ingredients in a small bowl.

Heat oil in wok and toss in the garlic and ginger for 30 seconds. Add the pork and stir-fry 2 minutes. Toss in the green onions briefly and then pour in the sauce. Stir and toss until sauce is heated through.

ORANGE AND HONEY PORK AND GREEN BEAN TOSS

Serves 4.

1-inch piece fresh ginger
1 pound thin green beans
1 pork tenderloin
2 tablespoons soy sauce
2 tablespoons honey
1/4 teaspoon crushed red pepper flakes
1 tablespoon vegetable oil

Sauce: 1/3 cup fresh orange juice
1 teaspoon rice vinegar
1 teaspoon cornstarch
1 teaspoon grated orange zest
1 clove garlic

Peel ginger and mince. Trim green beans and cut in half crosswise. Peel and mince garlic. Trim pork of all fat and silver skin and slice. Cut slices into thin strips. Combine ginger, soy sauce, honey and red pepper flakes and toss with pork. Let stand 30 minutes. Drop green beans in a pot of boiling water and cook 4 to 6 minutes until tender. Rinse in cold water to stop cooking.

Heat oil in a wok over medium high heat. Add pork, reserving marinade in dish. Cook until done, about 5 minutes. Add green beans and toss to warm. Add reserved marinade and sauce ingredients and cook until thickened. Season with salt and pepper and serve immediately.

ITALIAN PORK STEW

Serves 4 to 6.

1/2 pound crimini mushrooms
1 medium onion
2 cloves garlic
6 sprigs Italian parsley
2 ounces sliced smoked ham
2 pounds boneless pork shoulder
1 (28-ounce) can diced Italian style tomatoes
1 cup dry red wine
1/2 teaspoon dried crumbled rosemary
1/2 teaspoon dried crumbled oregano
1/2 teaspoon dried crumbled thyme
2 (14-1/2 ounce) cans white beans, rinsed
and drained

Wipe mushrooms clean with a damp paper towel and cut in half. Dice onion. Peel garlic and mince. Mince parsley and set aside. Cut ham into medium dice. Trim pork of most fat and cut into 1-1/2-inch cubes. Place pork in a 4-quart pot and cook, covered, over medium high heat for about 5 minutes. Uncover the pan and boil until juices are almost gone; then cook, stirring often, until drippings are dark brown, 10 minutes.

Add mushrooms, onion and garlic to pork. Cook until onion is softened, stirring 4 to 5 minutes. Add tomatoes with juices, wine, ham, rosemary, oregano and thyme. Bring to a boil. Lower heat and simmer, covered, until meat is tender when pierced, about 1-1/2 hours. Stir in beans and heat through. Serve sprinkled with parsley.

CARAMELIZED CARNITAS

Serves 4.

1-1/2 pounds boneless pork shoulder
2 cloves garlic
3 green onions
2 tablespoons brown sugar
1 tablespoon Tequila
1 tablespoon molasses
1/2 teaspoon salt
1/4 teaspoon freshly ground pepper
1 cup water
8 corn tortillas
Guacamole (see page 88)

Cut pork into 1-inch cubes, trimming off excess fat. Peel and mince garlic. Cut green onions across into thin slices and set aside.

Toss pork cubes with garlic, brown sugar, Tequila, molasses, salt and pepper and arrange in a single layer in a deep skillet. Add the water and bring to a simmer. Continue to cook until water is all gone, stirring occasionally. Continue to cook, stirring often to brown pork, about 45 minutes total cooking time.

Serves carnitas in warmed corn tortillas with guacamole and green onions.

PORK TENDERLOIN WITH ASIAN PLUM SAUCE

Serves 4.

**2 pork tenderloins (1-1/2 to 2 pounds total)
4 cloves garlic
1-inch piece fresh ginger
2 green onions
4 sprigs fresh cilantro
2 teaspoons grated orange zest
1/2 cup hoisin sauce
1/3 cup plum sauce
2 tablespoons sesame oil
2 tablespoons white vinegar
2 tablespoons oyster sauce
2 tablespoons soy sauce
2 tablespoons honey
2 tablespoons dry sherry
2 teaspoons Asian chili sauce**

Preheat the oven to 375 degrees. Trim pork of all fat and silverskin. Transfer to a parchment paper-lined baking sheet.

Peel garlic and ginger and mince. Chop green onions. Remove cilantro leaves from stems and mince. Combine garlic, ginger, green onions and cilantro with the remaining ingredients and spread half the sauce over the pork tenderloins. Roast the pork for 25 to 30 minutes or until the internal temperature reaches 155 degrees. Spread pork with remaining sauce and let stand 8 minutes before slicing and serving.

ITALIAN SAUSAGE SOUP

Serves 6 to 8.

**2 cloves garlic
1 medium onion
3/4 pound zucchini
1 yellow bell pepper
1 pound sweet Italian sausage links
1 tablespoon olive oil
1/2 cup dry white wine or vermouth
5 cups chicken broth
1 (16-ounce) can diced tomatoes
2 teaspoons dried basil
1 teaspoon dried oregano
Freshly ground pepper
1/2 cup pastini (tiny Italian soup pasta)
Freshly grated Romano cheese**

Peel garlic and mince. Chop onion. Cut zucchini and yellow pepper into medium dice. Place sausages in a saucepan and cover with cold water. Boil and then simmer for 10 minutes. Remove sausages and cool slightly. Slice sausages into 1/2- inch thick slices.

Heat olive oil in a large pot and add sliced sausages, onion and garlic. Sauté until onion is tender and sausages browned lightly, about 5 minutes. Add wine and stir until almost evaporated.
Stir in zucchini, pepper, broth, tomatoes with juices, basil, oregano and pepper to taste. Bring to a boil. Add the pastini and cook 20 minutes or until pasta and vegetables are tender. Serve with cheese.

CREAMY LINGUINE, BACON AND SUN-DRIED TOMATO TOSS

Serves 4 to 6.

3 large shallots
1/2 cup drained oil-packed sun-dried tomatoes
8 sprigs Italian parsley
8 slices bacon
1 tablespoon olive oil
1 cup whipping cream
1 pound linguine, cooked and drained
1/2 cup freshly grated Parmesan cheese
1/4 cup toasted pine nuts
More cheese for passing

Chop shallots. Cut sun-dried tomatoes in julienne strips. Remove parsley leaves and finely chop.

Chop bacon. Heat oil in a large heavy skillet over medium heat. Add the bacon and cook until beginning to color, about 6 minutes. Drain off fat. Add shallots and stir 2 minutes. Add cream and bring to a boil. Turn off the heat and add tomatoes.

Toss hot cooked linguine with sauce and 1/2 cup Parmesan. Season to taste with salt and pepper. Serve sprinkled with pine nuts and parsley, passing additional cheese separately.

MUSTARD MARINATED STEAK
WITH ARTICHOKE RELISH

Serves 4.

**4 cloves garlic
2 roasted red peppers
1 (6-ounce) jar marinated artichokes
2 tablespoons minced fresh basil
2 tablespoons balsamic vinegar
2 teaspoons Dijon mustard
1 teaspoon sugar
1 teaspoon salt
1/8 teaspoon freshly ground pepper
1/4 cup olive oil
1-1/2 pounds top sirloin, 1-inch thick**

Peel garlic and mince. Cut roasted peppers in julienne strips. Drain artichoke hearts and pat dry. Cut into medium dice. Stack basil leaves and mince. Whisk garlic, vinegar, mustard, sugar, salt and pepper in a small bowl. Whisk in olive oil. Remove 3 tablespoons to a medium bowl. Add the peppers, artichoke hearts and basil. Cover relish and leave at room temperature 1 hour. Pour remaining marinade over steak and let stand at room temperature 1 hour.

Preheat grill. Remove steak from marinade. Grill 6 to 8 minutes per side or to desired doneness. Let steak rest for 7 to 10 minutes before slicing across into thin strips. Serve steaks topped with relish.

GRILLED SIRLOIN WITH ROASTED GARLIC PORT SAUCE

Serves 4.

**6 cloves garlic
1/4 cup olive oil
1/2 teaspoon freshly ground pepper
1-3/4 pounds top sirloin
1/2 teaspoon salt
Roasted Garlic Port Sauce (see page 72)**

Peel garlic and mince. Stir garlic into olive oil with pepper. Pour over sirloin and let stand 1 hour at room temperature.

Season steak with salt and grill 6 to 8 minutes per side to desired doneness. Let steak rest for 7 to 10 minutes before slicing across into thin strips. Serve steaks topped with Roasted Garlic Port Sauce.

STEAK AND CORN SOFT TACOS

Serves 4.

1/2 bunch fresh cilantro
1 medium red onion
1 red bell pepper
1 pound top sirloin
1/4 cup olive oil
1-1/2 cups frozen corn, thawed
1/2 teaspoon ground cumin
1/2 teaspoon chili powder
4 flour tortillas
Guacamole (see page 88)
2 cups grated Cheddar cheese

Remove cilantro leaves and chop. Cover and set aside. Thinly slice onion lengthwise. Cut red pepper into julienne strips. Cut steak across the grain into 3 inch long thin strips.

Heat olive oil in a large skillet over medium heat. Add onion and red pepper and cook until very tender, about 8 minutes. Remove to a plate.

Raise the heat to medium high and add the streak strips. Toss until no longer pink, about 2 minutes. Return pepper and onions to skillet and add the corn, cumin and chili powder. Toss until heated through, seasoning with salt and pepper to taste. Serve in warmed tortillas topped with guacamole and grated cheese.

FILET MIGNON IN ZINFANDEL MUSHROOM SAUCE

Serves 4.

**3 sprigs Italian parsley
2 large shallots
1-1/2 pounds white button mushrooms
3 tablespoons unsalted butter, divided use
1 tablespoon flour
1 cup Zinfandel
1/2 cup ruby Port
1/2 cup beef broth
4 (6-ounce) filet mignons, 1-1/4 inches thick
Salt and pepper**

Remove parsley leaves and chop. Set aside. Slice shallots. Wipe mushrooms clean with a damp paper towel. Melt 2 tablespoons butter in a large nonstick skillet over medium-high heat. Add shallots; toss for 2 minutes. Add mushrooms and sauté until mushrooms are browned, about 10 minutes. Stir in flour. Add Zinfandel, Port, and broth. Boil until sauce thickens, stirring occasionally, about 10 minutes. Season with salt and pepper.

Melt remaining 1 tablespoon butter in another heavy large skillet over medium-high heat. Add steak to skillet and cook to desired doneness, about 4 minutes per side for medium-rare. Transfer steak to plates; do not clean skillet. Add mushroom sauce to skillet; bring to simmer, scraping up any browned bits. Spoon mushroom sauce over steaks and serve sprinkled with parsley.

CHILI ORANGE STEAK

Serves 4.

**6 sprigs fresh cilantro
2 cloves garlic, peeled
1 serrano chili
2/3 cup fresh orange juice
1 tablespoon chili powder
1 tablespoon olive oil
1-1/2 pounds skirt steak
1/2 cup sour cream**

Remove cilantro leaves from stems and chop. Cover and set aside. Peel garlic and trim stem end from chili and cut in half.

Place orange juice, chili powder, garlic, serrano and olive oil in a blender and pureé until smooth. Divide sauce in half and stir half into sour cream; cover and refrigerate. Pour remaining sauce over steak, turning to coat and marinate for 4 hours in the refrigerator.

Heat grill and cook steaks, 3 to 4 minutes per side or until cooked to desired doneness. Let stand 5 minutes and cut across the grain into thin strips. Serve topped with Sour Cream Sauce and sprinkled with cilantro.

MUSTARD MARINATED STEAK WITH ROASTED GARLIC AIOLI

Serves 6.

4 cloves garlic
2 large shallots
4 sprigs fresh thyme
1 sprig fresh rosemary
1/2 cup olive oil
1/3 cup red wine vinegar
4 tablespoons Dijon mustard
1 tablespoon freshly ground pepper
3 pounds top sirloin steaks,
(1-1/2 to 2 inches thick)

Roasted Garlic Aioli: 1 head garlic
1 tablespoon olive oil
1 tablespoon reserved steak marinade
1/4 cup mayonnaise

Peel and mince garlic. Peel shallots and finely chop. Remove thyme and rosemary leaves from stems and mince. Stir all into olive oil. Add the vinegar, mustard and pepper.   Reserve 1 tablespoon for aioli. Pour remaining over steak, cover and refrigerate 4 hours. Grill steak 6 to 8 minutes per side. Let rest and slice across the grain.

Cut top off whole head garlic and place on a sheet of foil. Drizzle with olive oil. Wrap tightly and roast at 400 degrees for 1 hour. Squeeze out garlic and mash. Mix garlic with reserved marinade and mayonnaise. Serve with steak.

TARRAGON PECAN CRUSTED SALMON

Serves 4.

**4 (6-ounce) salmon fillets
2 teaspoons orange zest
1/4 cup fresh orange juice
2 tablespoons olive oil
2 teaspoons minced fresh tarragon
1 tablespoon Dijon mustard
1 tablespoon butter, melted
1 teaspoon honey
1/4 cup fine dry breadcrumbs
1/4 cup finely chopped pecans
2 teaspoons minced Italian parsley
2 teaspoons minced fresh tarragon**

Place fish in a shallow dish. Whisk together orange zest, orange juice, olive oil and 2 teaspoons tarragon. Pour over fish, turning to coat. Marinate in refrigerator for 1 hour.

Preheat oven to 425 degrees. In a small dish combine mustard, melted butter and honey. In another dish combine breadcrumbs, pecans, parsley and remaining 2 teaspoons tarragon. Remove salmon from marinade and arrange on a parchment lined baking sheet. Brush with mustard mixture and coat with crumb mixture, pressing crumbs gently to coat. Bake for 12 to 16 minutes or until fish is cooked.

BAKED SALMON WITH AN OLIVE CRUST

Serves 4.

1/2 cup Kalamata olives
1/4 cup oil-packed sun-dried tomatoes, drained
3 cloves garlic
3 sprigs fresh thyme
1 sprig fresh rosemary
2 tablespoons olive oil
3 tablespoons Dijon mustard
1 cup panko (Japanese breadcrumbs)
4 (5 to 6 ounce) salmon fillets

Finely chop the olives and sun-dried tomatoes. Peel garlic and mince. Remove thyme and rosemary leaves from stems and mince.

In a medium bowl combine the olives, sun-dried tomatoes, garlic, thyme, rosemary, olive oil and 2 teaspoons mustard. Toss in the breadcrumbs.

Preheat oven to 400 degrees. Arrange salmon fillets on a parchment lined baking sheet. Spread with remaining mustard and mound breadcrumb mixture on top. Bake until salmon is just done in center, 12 to 15 minutes.

DEVILED SALMON WITH CAPERS

Serves 4.

2 cloves garlic
3 tablespoons capers, rinsed and drained
1 lemon
4 tablespoons Dijon mustard
4 (6-ounce) salmon fillets

Peel garlic and mince. Coarsely chop the capers. Cut the lemon in half. Cut one half into 4 wedges and squeeze the other half to make 1 teaspoon juice.

Preheat broiler. Stir together the garlic, capers, lemon juice and mustard. Arrange salmon fillets on a broiler pan and broil for 4 minutes. Carefully turn fillet over and spread with mustard mixture. Broil 5 to 7 minutes longer or until salmon is cooked through.

PESTO CRUMB TOPPED HALIBUT

Serves 4.

**1 green onion
1 clove garlic
2 tablespoons prepared pesto sauce
1/4 cup mayonnaise
2 cups fresh breadcrumbs
4 (6-ounce) halibut fillets**

Trim green onion and mince. Peel and mince garlic. Stir green onion and garlic into pesto and stir that mixture into the mayonnaise.

Preheat oven to 375 degrees. Arrange halibut on a parchment-lined baking sheet. Spread the top of each halibut fillet with 1/4 of the pesto mixture. Mound the breadcrumbs on top. Bake halibut for 18 minutes or until cooked through and the breadcrumbs are golden.

HALIBUT IN ASIAN BLACK BEAN GINGER SAUCE

Serves 6.

1 green onion
4 sprigs fresh cilantro
2-inch piece fresh ginger
3 cloves garlic
6 ounces fresh shiitake mushrooms
4 tablespoons vegetable oil, divided use
3 tablespoons Asian sesame oil
3 tablespoons dry white wine
4 tablespoons soy sauce
1-1/2 tablespoons Asian black bean garlic sauce
1-1/2 tablespoons hoisin sauce
1-1/2 tablespoons brown sugar
1-1/2 cups chicken broth
1 teaspoon freshly ground pepper
6 (6-ounce) halibut fillets
2 tablespoons unsalted butter

Trim green onion and mince. Remove cilantro leaves and mince. Peel ginger and garlic and mince. Wipe mushrooms clean with a damp paper towel, remove the stems and slice.

In a large skillet over medium heat, heat 2 tablespoons vegetable oil and sesame oil and add half the ginger and garlic and toss for 1 minute. Add the wine, soy sauce, black bean sauce, hoisin sauce, brown sugar, broth and pepper and cook for 3 minutes.

Heat remaining 2 tablespoons oil in a small skillet. Add the remaining ginger and garlic and mushrooms; sauté for 4 to 5 minutes or until softened and wilted. Set aside.

Add the fish fillets to the sauce in the large skillet and turn to coat with the sauce. Cover and simmer for 4 minutes. Turn fillets over, cover and continue cooking for 3 to 4 minutes. Remove fish with a slotted spoon to serving plates. Stir in mushrooms and butter until butter dissolves. Spoon sauce and mushrooms over fish and sprinkle with green onions and cilantro.

SCAMPI WITH RED PEPPERS

Serves 6.

**1 small bunch fresh basil
2 red bell peppers
2 large shallots
1 head garlic
1/4 cup unsalted butter
1/4 cup drained and rinsed capers
2 pounds large uncooked shrimp, cleaned**

Stack basil leaves and cut across into thin strips. Set aside. Cut red peppers into batonnet strips. Finely chop shallots. Peel garlic cloves and mince to make 1/4 cup.

Melt butter in a heavy large skillet over medium high heat. Add bell peppers, shallots and garlic and sauté until shallots begin to soften, about 4 minutes. Mix in capers. Transfer mixture to a large baking dish.

Preheat oven to 450 degrees. Mix shrimp into vegetables and bake until shrimp are cooked through, stirring occasionally, about 15 minutes. Sprinkle with basil.

SHRIMP AND CORN CHOWDER

Serves 4.

4 sprigs fresh parsley
2 green onions
1 medium onion
1 large potato
2 slices bacon, chopped
2 tablespoons unsalted butter
1 bay leaf
2 tablespoons flour
1/4 cup dry white wine or vermouth
3 cups chicken broth
1 cup half and half
1-1/2 cups fresh or frozen corn, thawed
1/2 pound raw shrimp, cleaned

Remove parsley leaves from stems and chop. Trim green onions and chop. Set both aside. Chop onion. Peel potato and cut into 1/2-inch cubes. Chop bacon.

Melt butter in a large pot over medium heat. Add bacon and cook until crispy. Add onion, potato and bay leaf. Cook about 5 minutes, stirring often. Stir in flour, then stir in wine and broth. Bring to a boil. Reduce heat, cover and simmer 20 minutes or until potatoes are tender. Add half and half and corn and return to a simmer and cook 5 minutes.

Meanwhile, cut shrimp down the back lengthwise into two pieces. Stir the shrimp into the chowder and simmer until shrimp turn pink, about 3 minutes. Stir in parsley and green onions and serve.

The Art of the KNIFE

The Art of the KNIFE

DESSERTS

SWEET FRUIT SALAD IN A WATERMELON BASKET

Serves 8 to 10.

**8 to 10 cups mixed fresh fruit, such as:
grapes, melon balls, blueberries, strawberries
and/or peaches and nectarines
1 whole watermelon**

**Dressing:
1/4 cup red currant jelly, melted
2 tablespoons raspberry vinegar
1 tablespoon sugar
1/2 teaspoon Dijon mustard
1/4 teaspoon paprika
1/2 teaspoon salt
1/2 cup vegetable oil**

Peel and cut up fruit that needs cutting into bite-size pieces. Combine all fruit in a large bowl.

Whisk together all dressing ingredients and toss with fruit. Cover and refrigerate no more than 3 hours.

Cut off top of watermelon and scoop out the melon and add to salad. Scallop cut the top edge and fill with fruit to serve.

The Art of the KNIFE

CREAMY CANTALOUPE MOUSSE

Serves 6 to 8.

1 large ripe cantaloupe
1/2 ripe honeydew melon
1 tablespoon unflavored gelatin
2 tablespoons cold water
1/2 cup sugar
1/4 teaspoon salt
1 teaspoon grated lemon zest
3 tablespoons fresh lemon juice
1 teaspoon vanilla
1 cup heavy whipping cream, whipped

Wash outside of cantaloupe well with soap and water. Cut in half and scoop out seeds. Cut half the cantaloupe into chunks and pureé to make 1-1/2 cups. Cut the remaining cantaloupe into balls or dice; cover and refrigerate. Peel honeydew melon and cut into thin wedges. Cover and refrigerate.

For mousse, stir gelatin into water in a 2 cups glass measuring cup. Let stand 5 minutes to firm up. Heat in the microwave on HIGH for 30 seconds to melt. Stir gelatin into cantaloupe pureé. Stir in sugar, salt, lemon zest and juice and vanilla. Cover and chill until partially set.

With mixer whip melon mixture until light and fluffy. Chill until mixture mounds slightly. Fold in whipped cream and reserved melon balls. Chill until set, about 4 hours. Serve spooned over honeydew melon slices.

APPLE GALETTE WITH ALMONDS

Serves 6 to 8.

4 medium Granny Smith apples
1/2 teaspoon almond extract
2/3 cup sugar
3 tablespoons flour
1 sheet frozen puff pastry, thawed
3 tablespoons cold butter, cut up
1/2 cup apricot preserves
1 tablespoon brandy
1/2 cup toasted sliced almonds

Preheat oven to 375 degrees. Peel apples and slice into 1/2-inch thick slices. Toss apples with almond extract. Combine sugar and flour and toss with apples.

Roll out the puff-pastry and cut to make an 11 inch circle. Transfer pastry to a parchment lined baking sheet. Arrange apples in a single layer in a circular pattern to completely cover pastry. Dot top with butter. Bake for 40 minutes or until apples are tender.
Heat apricot preserves in a small saucepan until melted. Strain preserves and stir in brandy. Brush over apples to glaze. Immediately sprinkle with toasted almonds. Let cool 10 minutes and cut into wedges to serve.

APPLE CRISP PIZZA

Serves 6 to 8.

**4 medium Granny Smith apples
2/3 cup sugar
3 tablespoons flour
1 teaspoon ground cinnamon
1 sheet frozen puff pastry, thawed
1/2 cup caramel ice cream topping
Vanilla ice cream**

**Topping:
1/2 cup flour
1/3 cup brown sugar
1/3 cup rolled oats
1 teaspoon ground cinnamon
1/4 cup unsalted butter, cut up**

Preheat oven to 375 degrees. Peel apples and slice into 1/2-inch thick slices. Toss with sugar, flour and cinnamon.

Roll and cut pastry to fit an 11 inch tart pan with removable bottom, folding the excess in to make the edges thicker. Fill pastry with the apples.

For topping, combine flour, brown sugar, oats, cinnamon and butter in a bowl and rub with fingers to make a crumbly mixture. Sprinkle over apples. Bake 35 to 40 minutes or until apples are tender. Remove to a rack and immediately drizzle the caramel topping over all. Serve warm with ice cream.

BRANDY PEAR TURNOVERS

Makes 8.

2 pounds firm ripe Anjou pears
1/4 cup dried cranberries
1/4 cup brandy
1/4 cup unsalted butter
2 tablespoons brown sugar
4 teaspoons fresh lemon juice
2 sheets frozen puff pastry, thawed
1/4 cup heavy cream
1/4 cup sugar
1 jar caramel sauce
Vanilla ice cream

Peel pears and cut into 1/2-inch cubes. Combine cranberries and brandy. Melt butter in a large nonstick skillet over medium high heat. Add brown sugar and cook until bubbly. Add pears and a pinch of salt. Cook and stir until pears are tender but not mushy. Add cranberries and brandy and keep cooking until syrupy. Stir in lemon juice and cool completely.

Preheat oven to 425 degrees. Cut each sheet of puff pastry into four equal squares. Divide filling among the 8 pastry squares and fold over to form a triangle, pressing edges together and using a fork to crimp. Transfer to a parchment lined baking sheet and brush with cream and sprinkle with sugar. Bake until deep golden brown, 18 to 22 minutes. Cool a few minutes before serving drizzled with caramel sauce and topped with ice cream.

ORANGE GINGER BROWNIES

Makes 16.

1 cup pecans
4 ounces bittersweet chocolate
2 ounces crystallized ginger
1 cup unsalted butter
4 large eggs
1-1/4 cups sugar
2 teaspoons vanilla
1 tablespoon grated orange zest
1/2 teaspoon salt
1/2 cup flour
Vanilla ice cream

Preheat oven to 350 degrees. Toast pecans for 8 minutes. Let cool and then coarsely chop. Cut chocolate into small pieces. Cut ginger into fine dice.

Butter a 9 x 12 inch baking pan. Place chocolate in a bowl with the butter and melt on HIGH power in the microwave for 1-1/2 to 2 minutes, stirring after 1 minute. Cool to lukewarm.

Beat eggs and sugar with mixer until thick and light colored. Beat in chocolate mixture and then stir in vanilla, orange zest, ginger, salt and nuts. Fold in flour and spread in prepared pan. Bake for 20 to 25 minutes or until just set in center. Cool; cut into squares and serve with ice cream.

MEXICAN CHOCOLATE BROWNIES

Serves 8.

**4 ounces unsweetened chocolate
1/2 cup unsalted butter
1-1/4 cups golden brown sugar
1 tablespoon ground cinnamon
1/4 teaspoon salt
3 large eggs
1 teaspoon vanilla
3/4 cup flour
1 cup milk chocolate chips (6 ounces)
Vanilla or Cinnamon ice cream**

Chop chocolate into small pieces. Stir chocolate and butter in a heavy large saucepan over low heat until melted and smooth. Cool 5 minutes.

Preheat oven to 325 degrees. Butter an 8-inch round cake pan and line with parchment paper. Whisk sugar, cinnamon and salt into cooled chocolate mixture. Whisk in eggs, one at a time, then vanilla. Continue to whisk until batter is smooth. Add flour and stir just until blended. Stir in chocolate chips.

Pour batter into prepared pan, smoothing surface. Bake until tester inserted into center comes out with a few moist crumbs attached, 25 to 30 minutes. Cool completely in pan on rack. Cut into wedges to serve with ice cream.

ENGLISH TOFFEE BROWNIES

Makes 16.

**5 (1.4-ounce) Heath English toffee
candy bars
1 cup walnut pieces
3 ounces unsweetened chocolate
1/4 cup unsalted butter
1/4 cup all purpose flour
1/4 teaspoon salt
1/4 teaspoon baking soda
1-2/3 cups sugar
3 large eggs
1 teaspoon vanilla extract**

Chop candy bars and set aside. Butter and flour a 13x9x2-inch metal baking pan.

Preheat oven to 350°F. Place walnuts in a pan and bake for 8 minutes. Chop nuts. Chop chocolate. Stir butter and chocolate in heavy small saucepan over low heat until melted and smooth. Cool to lukewarm. Whisk flour, salt, and baking soda in small bowl to blend.

Using electric mixer, beat sugar, eggs, and vanilla in large bowl until thick and light colored, about 3 minutes. Beat in chocolate mixture, then flour mixture. Fold in walnuts. Transfer to pan. Bake brownies 28 minutes or until set in center. Sprinkle brownies evenly with chopped toffee bars. Cut into squares.

WALNUT TORTE WITH MOCHA CREAM TOPPING

Serves 8.

1 cup walnuts
1 cup graham cracker crumbs
3 egg whites
1/8 teaspoon cream of tartar
1 teaspoon baking powder
1 cup sugar

Mocha Cream:
1 cup heavy cream
2 tablespoon powdered sugar
1 teaspoon instant espresso
1 tablespoon Kahlua or 1/2 teaspoon vanilla

Preheat oven to 350 degrees. Butter and flour a 9 inch pie plate. Finely chop the walnuts and combine with graham crackers. Beat egg whites with cream of tartar until soft peaks form. Slowly beat in the baking powder and then the sugar 1 tablespoon at a time. The meringue may be more syrupy than usual. Fold in the graham cracker crumbs and nuts. Spread in pie plate. Bake for 30 minutes or until puffed and set. Cool several hours on a rack.

One or two hours before serving whip cream with powdered sugar, espresso and Kahlua until stiff. Spread over torte and chill until serving time.